The Jockey on the Horse

The Jockey on the Horse

A Creative's Guide to AI: How to Thrive and Increase Creativity in the Age of AI

Nova Lorraine

Copyright © 2024 by Nova Lorraine

All rights reserved. No part of this book may be reproduced in any manner whatsoever without written permission except in the case of brief quotations embodied in critical articles and reviews.

First Edition: April 2024 Cover design by Nova Lorraine
Content Consultant: Murray Blehart
Interior design by Kristina Liburd
Printed in the United States of America

CONTENTS

Introduction

Part I: The AI Revolution in Creativity

1 Unleashing Creativity

2 Nova Lorraine – From Psychologist to AI and WEB3 Innovator

3 Understanding AI – What It Is and Why It Matters

4 AI Capabilities and Limitations

5 Unravelling the AI Ethics Dilemma

6 The Race Begins – AI Across Industries

7 AI's Impact on Creative Industries

8 AI Opportunities in Visual Arts and Design

9 AI And Music

10 AI And Writing

Part II: Future of Fashion and the Creative Economy

11 Fashion and AI – A Strong Use Case of an Industry Benefiting from AI

12 AI, Web3 and Fashion

13 The Web3 Connection – A Deeper Dive with Fashion as a Use Case

14 Shaping Fashion's Future - Blending My Designs with New Tech

Part III: Career Transitions, Mastering Change, and Creating Growth

15 Job Jitters – Navigating Career Changes in the AI Era

16 Managing Change, Uncertainty and Anxiety

17 Embracing the Uncertain Future

18 Skills for Staying Ahead

19 The Future of Work – Humans and AI Hand in Hand

20 Educating for Tomorrow – My Vision

21 Beyond Fear - Positive Narratives Around AI

22 Embracing the Uncertain Future

23 Cultivating the Abundant Mindset

24 Boosting Creativity and Possibility Thinking

Part IV: Exercises and Activities

25 Reflections and Exercises: Building Resilience and a Positive Mindset

26 Reflection Activities for Optimizing a Positive Mindset

27 Exercises and Reflections to Direct the Future

28 Supplemental Exercises for Future Mapping in and Out of the Office

29 Your Interactive Guide to Harness Generative AI

30 Practical Exercises for Future-Ready Learning

31 Cultivating Abundance: Reflection and Practice

Part V: AI and the New Creative Process from Fashion to Music and Beyond

32 The Creative Toolbox: AI Tools for Fashion, Visual Arts, Writing, and Beyond

33 The Future of AI is Hybrid

34 The Final Stretch - Sustaining Creativity and Success

CITATIONS

About The Author

ACKNOWLEDGMENTS

This book is a tribute to the supernova potential within all of us. Here is to those that face the future with a blend of curiosity, caution, and courage.

To my dear family, who has always been my anchor and inspiration, your endless support and belief in my dreams have made this journey both rewarding and inspiring.

To my colleagues and peers, your relentless drive to push the boundaries of what's possible is empowering.

A special thanks to the creative minds and brave souls who are ethically shaping the world of AI and Web3. Your innovations and perspectives pave the way for a future where technology enhances humanity, rather than diminishing it.

To my readers, thank you for taking this adventure with me. Your desire to explore new possibilities and challenge the status quo is the true driving force forward. May "The Jockey on the Horse" serve as a compass in your journey to maximize creativity, wealth, and wellbeing in the Age of AI.

And finally, to the future generations who will inherit this digital world, this book is for you. May you ride the horse of technological advancement with grace and perseverance, navigating through the challenges and opportunities it presents with an abundant mindset that fosters growth, innovation, and harmony.

Yours Truly,
Nova Lorraine

Dear Fellow Creative,

I was inspired to write this book to help others more easily transition into the digital age. From psychology to fashion to AI and emerging technology, my journey has been one of continuous learning and having an abundance mindset.

This is what is needed to take on this era of radical change with grace and ease. It is what is needed to learn, upskill and co-create in the Age of AI. We are at a pivotal moment where we, as creatives, inventors, and entrepreneurs can help steer the horse in a direction that benefits our personal and professional growth, as well as that of humankind.

Let's have our voices, creations, and positive intentions be what drives the horse forward, not fear or anxiety. We have a choice in how and what we create with AI. Let The Jockey and the Horse be your guide on this new journey into AI and how to maximize it for increase creativity, revenue, and wellbeing.

Yours Truly,

Nova

Introduction

Opening Thoughts

Imagine you're a jockey. Your horse is AI: powerful, swift, and ready to race towards the future. How do you prepare? Do you tighten the reins with anxiety and fear, or do you embrace the sprint, steering with confidence and skill? In "The Jockey on the Horse," we'll explore how to ride this wave of change with grace and foresight.

As an award-winning futurist, fashion designer, author, and global speaker, I've witnessed the blossoming relationship between creativity and technology. It's a masterpiece of potential, and AI is the climax that could complement or disrupt the melody of human creativity.

The Promise of AI: A Partnership of Potential

Artificial Intelligence is not just a tool; it's a force of nature, stretching the boundaries of our imagination. It's a partner in our expression of creativity, offering us new opportunities and possibilities we couldn't achieve alone. Fei-Fei Li of Stanford University puts it aptly: "AI will be one of the most significant partners in our history of human invention" (Li, 2018).

Education: Choreographing the Dance with AI

Education is the guide that must teach us the new steps. It's not about memorizing the choreography; it's about understanding the rhythm of AI. We must move beyond fear, as the Brookings Institution reminds us that the skills of the future are human skills – "creativity, empathy, and complex communication" (West, 2018). This book will guide you through rethinking education, not as a series of tests, but as a lifelong journey of learning and adaptation.

Creativity and AI: The Duet of the Century

Creativity is not a solo act; it's a duet with technology. As we forge this partnership, let's remember that our human touch, our genius, and our imagination are what will make this duet a perfect one. The World Economic Forum asserts that "human creativity is the key to unlocking the potential of AI" (Schwab, 2018). Together, we'll explore how to keep our creative muscles flexed and ready to perform with AI as our partner.

Policy and AI: Setting the Stage for Harmony

Policy is the platform where our dance with AI will play out. If done right, we will ensure that every participant has a chance to shine. The Future of Jobs Report by the World Economic Forum projects that "97 million new roles may emerge that are more adapted to the new division of labor between humans, machines, and algorithms" (WEF, 2020). This book will discuss how policy can nurture the potential of AI while protecting and empowering the human spirit.

Embracing for the Race

I've always believed in the power of visionaries to shape the future. This book is my vision for you: to become a jockey who not only stays ahead with AI but also co-creates a future where every race is worth running. Together, let's embrace the race and ride towards a not-too-far time that is filled with success and creativity.

So, hold the reins, feel the power beneath you, and let's stride into the future, where AI is our reliable friend, and the track ahead is ours to define and shape.

Part I: The AI Revolution in Creativity

1 Unleashing Creativity

The AI Revolution in Creative Industries
A friend of mine recently asked me, "How did you go about getting your first book, *Unleash Your SuperNova* published?" I stated matter-of-factly, "It had been in the making for years, and then with the right factors lining up, such as a self-imposed hard deadline, entering an author-to-agent pitch session, and landing the right literary agent were the final pieces that helped it come together."

As the words were coming out of my mouth, I knew I needed to then address how different the journey has been for my newest book, *The Jockey on the Horse*. I didn't want to underestimate the preparation, research, time, determination, teamwork, and "stick to it" mindset that was needed for it all to come together for my first book, especially during a pandemic. However, I realized that at that moment, I was describing what it took and often takes for a creative to bring an idea to life.

Nowadays, things are radically different, thanks to emerging technology, and more specifically Artificial Intelligence, aka AI.

My first book, *Unleash Your SuperNova*, was always inside of me. Truthfully, my life is the backdrop to the words on each page. As I would experience one life-altering moment after another and then choose to share it with a friend or stranger that cared to listen, I would often hear - as the last words were uttered out of my mouth, "You should write that down." "Your story was so inspiring, and it can really help people." Those words were repeated over and over again until one day, I took them to heart and had the aha moment I needed to commit to what seemed an elusive feat.

I knew deep down that instead of casually sharing my stories for entertainment, to sometimes just make myself chuckle – even with the tales that ended so badly – I could collect them in a way that could share light on an incredible journey of creative entrepreneurship. I would help others navigate the rollercoaster ride we call life, as we embark on a pursuit of happiness through the efforts of turning our passions into profit.

I felt that although many books exist about entrepreneurship, not many describe the good, the bad, and the ugly of our unpredictable daily reality. Even worse, less talked about the tools needed for a designer, writer, photographer, techie, architect, or artist for example, to navigate the journey of staying creative and not burning out, on this marathon of entrepreneurship.

A different origin story

This book has a different origin story, one that was inspired by my last few years dedicating my time and energy to educating emerging tech enthusiasts across industries on its impact on work, education, fashion, and creativity. With the rapid evolution of AI, which is often spoken about in my podcast, *AI for Creatives*, where, alongside my Co-Host Kamilah Sanders, I speak of the intersection of AI and creativity, and its impact on humanity.

From AI-generated images to soon AI-generated feature films, AI will continue to redefine workflows within industries, the definition of creativity, and how things are made and experienced. With this insight, I felt a strong need to gather this information in one place to empower creators, artists, and entrepreneurs with the many ways AI can unleash our ability to create and expand our imaginations.

I also share how an abundance mindset will help us weather the rollercoaster of disruption and transformation that will come from the rapid integration of AI in our daily work and personal lives. *The Jockey on the Horse* is about thriving, innovating, and leading in the Age of AI.

The impact of AI on creative industries

In this introductory chapter, we embark on a journey to explore the profound impact of artificial intelligence (AI) on creative industries. The convergence of human creativity and AI innovation has ushered in a new era of possibilities, redefining the way we conceive, produce, and experience art, design, music, writing, and various other forms of creative expression. As we delve into the transformative power of AI in unleashing creativity, we will navigate through its capabilities, limitations, and the unprecedented opportunities it presents for creatives and entrepreneurs.

The creative process has always been a deeply personal and introspective endeavor, rooted in the unique experiences, emotions, and perspectives of individuals. As we reflect on the evolution of our creative journeys, we are confronted with the realization that our stories are not just isolated narratives, but interconnected ribbons in the rich assortment of human expression. Each moment of inspiration, every triumph and setback, and the relentless pursuit of turning our creative visions into tangible realities have shaped the collective narrative of creative entrepreneurship.

The emergence of AI as a formidable ally in the realm of creativity has sparked a paradigm shift, challenging conventional notions of authorship, artistic innovation, and the boundaries of human imagination. The fusion of human ingenuity with AI's computational prowess has unlocked new frontiers in creative exploration, enabling us to push beyond the confines of traditional artistic methodologies and explore uncharted territories of expression.

As we embark on this exploration of AI's impact on creative industries, we are called to embrace the duality of its influence - the awe-inspiring potential it holds to amplify our creative capabilities and the nuanced considerations it demands in navigating the ethical, societal, and personal dimensions of its integration into our creative processes.

The chapters that follow will serve as a compass, guiding us through the multifaceted landscape of AI in creative industries, offering insights, inspiration, and practical wisdom to empower creatives and entrepreneurs in harnessing the full potential of AI while preserving the essence of human creativity.

Shedding light on the path

Through candid reflections on my own creative journey and the invaluable lessons learned from navigating the ever-evolving terrain of creative entrepreneurship, I aspire to shed light on the path for fellow creatives and entrepreneurs. This book is an invitation to embark on a transformative journey - a journey that celebrates the resilience, innovation, and unwavering spirit of creatives in embracing the AI revolution and charting a course toward a future where creativity knows no bounds.

As we ride into this uncharted territory, Let's embrace the infinite possibilities that await us, and may this exploration ignite a spark of inspiration within each reader, propelling them towards new horizons of creative expression and entrepreneurial success.

In the subsequent chapters, we will delve into the intricacies of AI's creative capabilities, its impact on diverse creative domains such as visual arts, music, writing, and design, and the profound implications it holds for shaping the future of creative entrepreneurship. We will also navigate through the ethical considerations, practical insights, and transformative potential of AI in fostering a thriving ecosystem for creatives and entrepreneurs.

The journey that lies ahead is one of discovery, growth, and empowerment - an odyssey that transcends the boundaries of conventional wisdom and invites us to reimagine the possibilities of human-AI collaboration in shaping a future where creativity flourishes in harmony with technological innovation.

2 Nova Lorraine – From Psychologist to AI and WEB3 Innovator

"The only way to discover the limits of the possible is to go beyond them into the impossible." - ARTHUR C. CLARKE

In the journey of life, we often come across crossroads that compel us to choose between the comfort of the known and the pull of the unknown. A very pivotal point in my life, was when I decided to shift my career from the clinical world of psychology to the boundless realm of fashion design and, ultimately, to the visionary sphere of futurism.

As a doctoral candidate entrenched in the study of the human mind, I loved learning about the theoretical frameworks and the rich therapeutic techniques within clinical environments. Yet, I was lulled by a different song—a tune that drew me towards color, texture, and impact of design. It was a tune that I, at first, resisted but ultimately could not ignore.

The decision to embrace my true calling was not merely a career shift; it was a metamorphosis that would take me from the comforting cocoon of academia into the unpredictable world where creativity meets innovation. This chapter is a reflection of that transformation—a tale of overcoming fears, combining different worlds, and continually evolving into one's best self.

Overcoming Fears to Follow Your Destiny

Fear is a relentless guardian of the status quo, often holding us back from pursuing our true passions. I had to confront these fears head-on, challenging the inner voices that whispered of impracticality and potential failure. It was a battle against the grains of societal norms and the weight of traditional expectations.

But in this struggle, I found strength in the words of Amin Maalouf, who dared us to change everything by doing the one thing we feared most. For me, that meant embracing the unknown world of fashion—a domain I believed was my true home.

Fusing Intuition, Art, and Social Science

The intersection of psychology, art, and technology is a fertile ground for innovation. As I ventured into the world of fashion design, I discovered an intense connection between the insights from my psychological background and the visual expressions of fashion.

Neuroscience research has begun to unpack the complex ways in which our clothing choices reflect and influence our emotions, self-perception, and social dynamics. By incorporating this knowledge with the intuitive process of design, I began to see fashion as not just an art form, but as a powerful medium for psychological and social transformation.

Continually Reinventing Your Best Self

Life is an ongoing journey of self-discovery and reinvention. Each step we take opens new doors and reveals aspects of ourselves that we may not have known existed. As I delved deeper into the world of emerging technology, I learned that the key to thriving in a rapidly changing world is adaptability and a willingness to continually evolve.

By embracing the uncertainties of the future, especially in the face of AI and Web3, I aligned my creative endeavors with the trajectory of technological progress. This alignment has not only expanded my horizons but also positioned me to influence the dialogue around human-AI collaboration.

Rising Beyond Limiting Narratives

The narratives we tell ourselves can either limit our potential or empower us to achieve greatness. It is crucial to rewrite the stories that no longer serve us, breaking free from the constraints of outdated myths and self-imposed limitations.

As I transitioned from psychologist to futurist, I learned to create a new narrative, one that celebrated the merging of my diverse interests and experiences. This new story empowered me to redefine success on my own terms and to contribute to the world in a way that only I could.

Embracing the Unknowns of Career Evolution

The path from psychologist to creative technologist has not been linear, it has been an ever-expanding journey of exploration and discovery. Each experience has been an opportunity for growth, with every twist and turn contributing to a larger pattern of personal and professional evolution.

While on our individual paths, the lessons of the past merge with the possibilities of the future, creating a rich landscape for continual learning and growth. It is a reminder that our careers are not just a series of jobs or titles but a reflection of our evolving identity and purpose.

The Abundance Mindset: Embracing the Future Without Fear

In the heart of every visionary lies an abundance mindset—an unwavering belief in the limitless potential of the future. As I transitioned from the predictability of psychology to the fluidity of fashion and futurism, I realized that to thrive in the age of AI and the emerging technology within Web3, one must see the future not as a threat, but as an expansive sea of possibilities.

The fear of the future often stems from a scarcity mindset, a belief that change will reduce what we have or who we are. Yet, the opposite is true. Like the universe, our potential is ever-expanding, infinite in its scope. The age of AI is not a time for trepidation but for tremendous opportunity, for creativity, for innovation, and for transforming society for the better.

AI is not just a technological advancement; it's a canvas for our imagination, a partner in our creative endeavors, and a catalyst for growth. It amplifies our abilities, extends our reach, and frees us from mundane tasks, allowing us to dream bigger and achieve more. The fusion of human intuition with AI's capabilities can usher in an era of unprecedented creativity and innovation.

Transformation as a Catalyst for Growth

Transformation is the alchemy of the soul, turning the leaden weight of our past fears into the gold of future possibilities. My own transformation taught me that change is not something to resist but to embrace as a natural progression of life's journey.

As a psychologist, I was trained to help others navigate the complexities of change. Yet, it was in my embrace of fashion and technology that I truly understood the transformative power of change. It was not just about changing careers but about changing perspectives, about seeing the world not as it is but as it could be.

The age of AI calls us to transform, to reimagine our roles in society, and to redefine what it means to be human in a world where machines can think. It challenges us to elevate our human qualities— creativity, empathy, and intuition—qualities that AI can enhance but not replicate.

An Abundant Future with AI

An abundant future is one in which technology and humanity coalesce, creating a synergy that elevates both. In this future, AI is not a competitor but a collaborator, a tool that we wield with intention and creativity.

The age of AI can be a golden era of human achievement if we approach it with the right mindset. By adopting an abundance mentality, we can leverage AI to address some of the world's most pressing challenges, to amplify human ingenuity, and to foster a culture of innovation and inclusivity.

Our future with AI should be guided by the principles of ethical design, sustainability, and the betterment of humanity. We must shape AI to reflect the best of us, to serve the common good, and to ensure that the benefits of technology are shared by all.

The Mandala of Our Shared Humanity

As we stand at the cusp of the AI revolution, we must remember that at the center of this mandala is our shared humanity. It is our values, our dreams, and our collective aspirations that should guide the development and deployment of AI.

The mandala is a reminder that everything is interconnected. Our choices, our actions, and our attitudes toward AI will shape not only our own future but the future of all life on this planet. We must choose wisely, act compassionately, and dream boldly.

I have journeyed from the depths of the human psyche to the cutting edge of technology, and I have seen the potential for a future filled with abundance, transformation, and hope. I invite you, the reader, to join me in this journey, to embrace the age of AI with an abundant mindset, to see transformation as a catalyst for growth, and to work towards a future that reflects the best of our shared humanity.

In the words of R. Buckminster Fuller, "We are called to be architects of the future, not its victims." Together, Let's build a future that is abundant, inclusive, and vibrant—a future where AI serves as a bridge to a world of limitless possibilities.

JOCKEY ON THE HORSE

3 Understanding AI – What It Is and Why It Matters

Brief History and Definition of AI

"AI is the most profound technology we have ever created," stated Joon Yun, President of Palo Alto Longevity Prize. Artificial intelligence, or AI, refers to computer systems and machines that can perform tasks typically requiring human cognitive abilities like visual perception, speech recognition, decision-making, and translation between languages (Popenici & Kerr, 2017).

The quest to create intelligent machines dates at least as far back as ancient Greek myths of Hephaestus, the god of technology who forged automatons to assist in his workshop. The term "artificial intelligence" itself was coined at an academic conference in 1956 when computer scientists proposed the possibility of machines being able to think and learn like humans. In the modern sense, AI is powered by algorithms and logical sets of rules for solving problems. These algorithms enable AI systems to analyze data, identify patterns, learn from experience, and ultimately make decisions or predictions (Jumper et al., 2022).

When I started my journey in medicine and then pivoted to fashion, I never thought I would collaborate with AI, in particular Generative AI to create art, conceptualize ideas, and build tools for well-being. The first tool that kicked off this AI, was MidJourney, an image generator. Since then, I have added many AI tools in my toolbox. Before Generative AI, most of us were unaware of how much AI has powered so many devices that have become part of our everyday routines.

From digital assistants like Siri to autonomous vehicles to personalized movie recommendations on Netflix, AI is becoming integrated across industries. As AI capabilities continue to rapidly improve, it shows the potential to greatly enhance human skills while raising ethical considerations on issues like privacy and bias.

The Jockey's Toolkit: Understanding AI Basics

"I visualize a time when we will be to robots what dogs are to humans, and I'm rooting for the machines." – Claude Shannon, mathematician and "father of information theory"

Artificial intelligence (AI) remains shrouded behind an aura of mystery for many, summoning sci-fi visions of omnipotent machines either benevolently accommodating to our every whim, or maliciously turning against unfortunate humans in a quest for domination.

Yet beyond such imaginative speculation lies the reality – AI comprises pragmatic digital tools serving useful, often everyday functions to strengthen knowledge work, commerce, and more. Familiarizing ourselves with essential AI concepts and terminology demystifies this transformative technology, empowering more informed, thoughtful adoption.

Defining Artificial Intelligence

AI refers to computerized systems exhibiting human-like intelligence. Incorporating capabilities like visual perception, speech recognition, decision-making, and language translation, AI can perform tasks typically requiring human cognition and senses (Rouse, 2022).

Sub-Fields and Specializations

Just as medical practice contains specialized niches like surgery, pediatrics, and neurology, AI similarly comprises particular sub-fields, including:

- **Machine Learning** – Algorithms "learn" to improve at tasks independently via exposure to training data sets vs relying solely on hardcoded programming (Rao, 2022)
- **Computer Vision** – Automated processing and analysis of visual data like digital images and videos (IBM Cloud Education, 2022)
- **Natural Language Processing** – Computer interpretation and generation of human languages, facilitating AI apps like virtual assistants and chatbots (Reddy, 2021)
- **Robotics** – Development of mechanical machines capable of carrying out complex actions with speed, precision, and ethics (The Royal Society, 2017)

Key AI Concepts and Terms

- **Algorithm** – Set of defined steps for solving problems or performing automated reasoning (Rouse, 2020)

- **Artificial Neural Networks** – Computing systems modeled after the biological brain's meshlike network of neuron cells and synapses. Key to modern AI innovations, especially in image recognition (IBM Cloud Education, 2022).
- **Automation** – Technologies performing tasks previously requiring human labor (Merriam-Webster, 2022)
- **Big Data** – Extensive complex data sets assessed by AI to reveal patterns, trends, and associations for improved decision-making, predictions, and processes (Rouse, 2021)
- **Cognitive Computing** – Computerized environments mimicking the workings of the human brain to interpret data just as people do (Rouse, 2019)
- **Ethics** – Moral principles guiding AI development and usage so innovations benefit society while minimizing harm (Bughin, 2022)
- **General Intelligence** – Ability to learn any intellectual task humans can perform. Also called artificial general intelligence (AGI) which does not yet exist (Edwards, 2022).
- **Singularity** – Theoretical point at which machine intelligence surpasses human abilities and redesigns itself recursively, creating runaway improvements (Walsh, 2022).

Bridging Digital Technologies

AI does not develop inside a vacuum. Rather, most AI tools harness or interface with other prominent digital innovations transforming society, including:

- **Cloud Computing** – On-demand delivery of IT resources via the Internet rather than local servers, providing access to shared pools of configurable resources (Reddy, 2021)
- **Big Data and Data Analytics** – Assessing expansive, complex datasets to uncover trends, associations, and insights that inform business decisions and AI functionality (Rouse, 2021)
- **The Internet of Things (IoT)** – Millions of internet-connected smart devices sending and receiving data using embedded sensors. Includes smart home assistants, health monitors, appliances, vehicles and more (Reddy, 2021).
- **5G** – Next-generation wireless connectivity allowing faster speeds, lower latency, and exponential capacity to manage expanding smart devices and AI apps (Reddy, 2021)

- **Quantum Computing** – Leveraging quantum mechanical phenomena like entanglement and superposition to realize unprecedented computing speeds/power to bolster areas like AI, financial modeling, weather prediction, particle physics, and astronomy (Sasaki, 2021).

Current and Future AI Applications

AI is already actively contributing across medicine, education, agriculture, finance, and more. In 2021 alone, global healthcare AI startups raised $4.9 billion as AI improves diagnostic accuracy and facilitates new therapeutic discoveries (Holmes et al., 2022).

In the near future, AI is expected to improve human creativity vs fully replace it by automating mundane tasks and providing sizeable data insights at incredible speed so people can focus more on innovation, impact, and personal growth (Daugherty & Wilson, 2018). AI also shows promise in helping address biases through auditing datasets and algorithms and then rectifying unfair impacts (Shankar et al., 2017).

As capabilities advance further, AI may even free up newfound "freedom time" for prioritizing family, passion projects, and rest according to experts like MIT research scientist Dr. Vivienne Ming. This prospect is especially exciting for busy entrepreneurs, multi-tasking moms, and extreme hobbyists. AI can truly be a game changer for improving well- being by offering back more quality time for many. As a mom of four, a serial entrepreneur, author, and international speaker, I am constantly seeking ways to balance the time I am giving to my creative pursuits and my family. I have already experienced many ways AI has added more time back in life by taking over some basic tasks and increasing work- flow efficiency.

Effect on Jobs and the Economy

The rise of AI will displace many routine jobs but also generate new specialized roles and even entirely new industries. A 2021 PwC survey estimates AI automation will replace 22% of jobs by 2030 and boost global GDP by $15 trillion in the same timeframe by improving productivity and enhancing consumption power (PwC, 2021).

This net positive effect echoes historical patterns seen in past technological revolutions like mechanized farming and electrification which unlocked newfound wealth for many, despite requiring workforce retraining. As manual jobs declined during these shifts, uniquely human skills became more crucial. MIT labor economist David Autor predicts this trend will continue in the AI age with a growing emphasis on expertise in engineering and creativity. Management scholar Richard Baldwin likewise forecasts that "human genius" abilities like design, empathy, and analysis will skyrocket in value through the 2020s.

Ethical Considerations

As AI gets embedded across high-stakes domains like healthcare, transportation, and finance, thoughtfully addressing ethical risks grows increasingly vital. Internationally, an "AI arms race" has emerged with superpowers aggressively competing to dominate AI advancement, raising valid concerns around misuse, unfair bias, lack of transparency, and more (Bughin et al., 2017).

Incorporating diverse perspectives into AI training data and intentionally engineering inclusive, accountable algorithms aligned to human values can help promote positive change rather than unintended losses as AI permeates society more deeply in the coming years (Whittaker et al., 2018). Carefully crafted policies and shared best practices around AI ethics will likewise help guide responsible progress.

Weaving these elements together enables an intelligent, responsive, and automated environment supporting sophisticated AI across domains like business, medicine, education, sustainability initiatives, and more.

Yet as digital transformation makes infrastructure smarter and society more convenient, we must balance progress with purpose, continuously considering technology's implications for people and the planet so innovation remains anchored by a strong ethical foundation.

4 AI Capabilities and Limitations

"With artificial intelligence, we are summoning the demon."
- ASTROPHYSICIST STEPHEN HAWKING ON EMERGING TECHNOLOGY

Exploring AI's Creative Capabilities

Artificial intelligence (AI) has significantly transformed the landscape of creative industries, offering a wide array of capabilities that have revolutionized the creative process. AI's role in creative industries is multifaceted, encompassing areas such as story generation, music composition, and character development. For instance, AI-powered tools like ChatGPT and Dabble Writer's Story Engine have emerged as powerful resources for writers, assisting in tasks such as creating story outlines, fleshing out chapters, and generating human-like text. These AI tools are designed to enhance creativity and increase writing efficiency, providing authors with a wealth of resources to streamline the writing process and bring their ideas to life.

As one writer expressed, "It can be used for just about anything writing-related. Some artists, including writers, are using it to help them brainstorm ideas, outline their work, or even generate entire chapters or stories". Additionally, AI has proven to be a valuable asset in music composition, with AI music generators offering creatives the ability to create easy tunes and explore new musical possibilities.

Furthermore, AI's capabilities extend to character development, with tools like NovelAI providing the ability to generate images to depict characters in fiction books. While AI has the potential to write high-quality fiction books, it is important to note that the heart of the story, its soul and essence, still comes from the human author. AI tools for book writing are designed to supercharge creativity, assisting authors in everything from character development to plot creation, while ensuring their unique voice and style remain the focal point.

Ultimately, AI's creative capabilities are reshaping the creative industries, offering a wealth of opportunities for collaboration and innovation. As AI continues to evolve, its potential to augment human creativity and streamline the creative process will undoubtedly play a pivotal role in the future of the arts.

In addition to writing, AI has also been utilized in other creative domains. For example, in the field of visual arts, AI has been employed to generate art and aid artists in their creative process. Tools like DeepArt and Runway ML allow artists to create unique pieces by leveraging AI algorithms that can generate images or assist in the artistic process. Moreover, AI's impact extends to music production, where it has been used to create new and innovative sounds. Artists and musicians have employed AI-generated music to explore novel compositions and push the boundaries of traditional music creation. These examples illustrate the diverse applications of AI in fostering creativity across various artistic disciplines.

AI has been increasingly utilized in filmmaking to enhance the creative process. AI solutions in video editing have drastically reduced production times and decreased the budget needed to fulfill filmmaking projects. By automating certain processes, AI frees up time for filmmakers to explore innovative ideas and experiment with storytelling techniques. AI tools have conjured the voices of iconic figures and are making waves in de-aging software that shaves decades off of actors, offering new storytelling possibilities to filmmakers of all levels.

The transformative impact of AI on filmmaking has led to efficiency, cost reduction, and immersive storytelling, making it an invaluable resource for filmmakers across the industry. Additionally, AI has made significant strides in the fashion industry, where it has been employed to revolutionize the way individuals work in fashion, fine art, broadcasting, and more. New forms of AI have made great differences in the way we work in fashion, offering innovative solutions for tasks such as content creation, design optimization, and personalized user experiences. Back to filmmaking, AI has also been used to generate scripts, storylines, and plot suggestions based on data and patterns derived from existing films and literary works.

AI's creative capabilities are continuously evolving and have already demonstrated their potential to significantly impact the creative industries. By leveraging AI-powered tools, creatives can enhance their artistic output, streamline their creative processes, and explore new frontiers of expression. As AI continues to advance, its role as a collaborative partner in the creative process will likely become even more pronounced, offering artists and creators unprecedented opportunities for innovation and artistic exploration.

Limitations and Ethical Considerations in AI Creativity

The use of AI in creative industries presents a myriad of ethical considerations and limitations that call for careful examination. One of the key ethical issues in AI for creativity is data responsibility and privacy. Data is the fuel for AI systems, as they rely on large datasets to generate novel and diverse content, and by providing insights, suggestions, and feedback. However, it can also raise ethical issues and dilemmas, such as data responsibility and privacy, fairness, and diversity, explainability and transparency, value alignment, and trust. The use of AI for creativity also raises ethical questions and challenges. How do we ensure that AI respects the values, rights, and dignity of human creators and consumers? How do we balance the benefits and risks of AI for creativity? How do we foster responsible and ethical use of AI for creativity? These critical questions require thoughtful consideration and robust ethical frameworks to guide the development and deployment of AI in creative industries.

Another significant ethical concern in the context of AI for creativity is the potential for bias and discrimination. AI systems are trained on large datasets, and if these datasets contain biases, the AI-generated content may reflect and perpetuate these biases. For example, in the realm of AI art, the generated content can be plagued with biases because the code relies on human input and a vast storehouse of reference images. This raises important questions about how to mitigate bias in AI-generated content and ensure that it upholds principles of fairness, diversity, and inclusivity.

Transparency and accountability are also central to the ethical considerations of AI for creativity. As AI systems become increasingly sophisticated, it is essential to develop explainable AI that helps characterize the model's fairness, accuracy, and potential bias. This is particularly important in creative industries, where the provenance of artistic content and the decision-making processes of AI systems must be transparent to ensure accountability and trust.

The issue of creativity and ownership in the context of AI-generated content is a complex and evolving ethical concern. When AI systems are used to generate artistic content, questions arise about who owns the content and who can commercialize it. The emerging issue of determining ownership of AI-generated art is still evolving as AI advances faster than regulators can keep up. This raises critical questions about intellectual property rights, copyright ownership, and the ethical implications of commercializing AI-generated content.

The ethical considerations of AI in creative industries are multifaceted and require a comprehensive approach to address. From data responsibility and privacy to bias and discrimination, transparency and accountability, and creativity and ownership, these ethical concerns must be carefully navigated to ensure that AI for creativity serves the common good of humanity, individuals, societies, and the arts. By proactively engaging with these concerns and fostering ongoing discussions, we can harness the incredible potential of AI while upholding ethical principles to shape a future that promotes human flourishing within the digital ecosystem.

5 Unravelling the AI Ethics Dilemma

As a Jamaican-born, first-generation college grad, with a passion for fairness, balance, and access, ethics is a top priority for me and what I create and disseminate. It's Stephen Hawking's poignant words serve as a strong call to the nuanced maze of artificial intelligence (AI) ethics. As AI's reach extends into important sectors—finance, justice, defense, healthcare, transportation— the collective conscience demands a shift towards increased ethical vigilance and risk mitigation.

The adoption of AI without a strong ethical compass poses a variety of risks. Biased decision-making algorithms could perpetuate inequality, intruding upon civil liberties (Whittaker et al., 2018). Privacy breaches through unchecked data collecting erode public trust, while the increase of disinformation via deep fakes distorts reality. Additionally, efforts for equal access are critical to ensure the masses aren't left behind.

Yet, amidst these challenges, pathways emerge that bring together AI's evolution with our cherished humanistic principles. Scholars like Harvard's Dr. Latanya Sweeney champion the cause for transparent design, a harmonious blend of efficiency and equity, steering clear of bias and power monopolies (Sweeney, 2021).

Globally, the adoption of foundational AI ethics norms from accountability to public understanding and awareness begins to sketch the outline of a socially conscious tech landscape. Technologists, too, are embracing a 'conscientious design' ethos, one that fosters accessibility, transparency, and impartiality (Jobin et al., 2019). A solid representation of diverse voices, the experiences of those most impacted by AI, contributes to a vision of innovation rooted in empowerment and inclusivity.

The key to nonthreatening AI advancement might lie within the realm of human relationships—the very sphere where technology, with its persistent march towards optimization, often disrupts. Visionaries suggest that protecting economic vitality and social harmony may hinge on redefining corporations as "public benefit institutions," responsible for harmonizing profits, environmental stewardship, and workforce wellbeing (Askell et al., 2021).

This reflection mirrors the timeless lesson that true progress comes not from data and algorithms alone but from the courageous intertwining of moral fiber and societal unity—an alchemy no AI can create. Herein lies the power of ethical human intent, directing technology with a compass attuned to uphold rights and dignity as the leading example of progress.

Preserving Meaning Amidst Dislocation

In the frenzy of AI-induced labor market upheavals, the future of entire societies may pivot on sustaining the subtle yet essential elements of meaning, trust, and community—elements often worn away by the singular pursuit of efficiency. In the end, our survival through periods of intense uncertainty may very well depend on the strength of our social bonds, an architecture no AI can replicate or replace.

With future possibilities burdened with both promise and peril as AI integration accelerates, our collective steering through this landscape becomes vital. Do we spiral into dystopian fears, or do we harness AI as an ally in crafting a future filled with justice? Our mindset, both purpose and perception, shapes our destiny.

Thriving Through Times of Transition

AI is not a harbinger of doom but a vessel of boundless potential. Retailers are already deploying AI to personalize shopping experiences and streamline supply chains. In creative realms, AI doesn't suppress artistry but rather, much like the camera did for painters, offers new canvases for expression. When used with intention, AI transforms from a blind force to a tool that amplifies our potential, fostering an ecosystem of innovation built on a strong foundation of ethics.

Therefore, as we take this journey into this uncharted territory, let's keep ethics as a priority, ensuring that our path toward progress remains true to our shared values. The goal is to work towards harmony, where technology serves humanity, and justice remains our guiding star.

Cultivating Collective Intelligence

The narrative we craft around AI will shape our experience of entering into this new era. Will we lead with fear of machine domination, or will we rise to meet AI as the catalyst for a renaissance of our prosperity? The mindset we nurture now will turn into the future we experience. We hold the power to impart emerging tools with a spirit of shared ethics and social benefit. Our task is not to withdraw from the unfamiliar but to shape it with a wisdom that inspires and unites.

Policy Shaping AI's Trajectory

It is through thoughtful advocacy and informed policy-making that we will set the boundaries for AI's role in society. Organizations like the AI Now Institute provide critical insights, guiding us toward a future where technology enhances rather than undermines our collective well-being.

As we pivot from legacy roles to emerging domains, supportive policy measures that foster education, skills development, and job transition will be crucial. By nurturing an environment that values human adaptability and resilience, we can ensure that the arrival of AI is marked not by obsolescence but by opportunity.

The most optimal vision of our shared future, every voice matters. It is only by giving equal importance to both innovation and human first principles, that we can move towards a future that values dignity, freedom, and human potential over profit.

Claude Shannon, a pivotal figure in the development of digital circuit design theory, once imagined a future where robots might assume roles similar to that of loyal canines to humans—an analogy underscoring the potential depth of AI's integration into our lives.

6 The Race Begins – AI Across Industries

"I visualize a time when we will be to robots what dogs are to humans."
- CLAUDE SHANNON, MATHEMATICIAN AND FATHER OF INFORMATION THEORY

The latest improvements in AI mark a huge shift across the economy. It can bring new levels of intelligence, automation, and flexibility into systems. This wave seeks to:

- Boost productivity
- Spark innovation
- Improve customer experiences

The goals are to make processes smoother, more quickly uncover new ideas, and strengthen interactions. AI's rise signifies a big lift across sectors.

Though some jobs may decline as AI grows smarter, with care it can boost what makes us human. Much as machines took over physical tasks in the Industrial Revolution, freeing people for more fulfilling roles, AI could relieve the repetition, leaving space for heightened creativity, vision, and purpose. Guided well, its rise could allow more of the philosophical and strategic - the very corners that comprise the human experience. This new companion holds the potential to elevate much of what we are.

AI now touches our everyday lives - from getting recommendations to talking to virtual helpers to riding in self-driving vehicles. As it spreads across culture and business, we must grasp how AI transforms each area. These lessons show how exponential tech can both enhance current tasks and illuminate new directions to explore. Tracking AI's imprint allows us to map its emerging role in the fabric of our existence.

AI in Retail and E-Commerce

In retail, AI enables a more personal shopper connection. Algorithms tailor suggestions and deals to each customer. Data analytics strategically guide pricing and inventory. Computer vision introduces cashier-less shopping and other seamless in-store experiences.

E-commerce, too, is transforming through AI. Chatbots boost customer interactions and sales. Generative tools craft targeted email campaigns and product descriptions.

As augmented and virtual reality advance, digital "try before you buy" grows commonplace. Customers can visualize furnishings in their spaces or clothing on their bodies. Combined with predictive AI, this ushers unprecedented convenience - anticipating consumer needs for restocking and signaling when to prompt repeat purchases. The result is the pinnacle of frictionless commerce.

AI in Finance

Robo-advisors are leading a finance renaissance, using AI to turn complex data into personalized investing strategies. These automated counselors expand access to asset management and risk planning once exclusive to the wealthy.

In trading, lightning-fast algorithms conduct millions of trans- actions seeking split-second advantages. Fraud systems also harness machine learning, dissecting data to uncover hidden criminal patterns and strengthen financial defenses.

Banking welcomes AI as an efficiency tool. Chatbots address com- mon questions while AI writing creates personalized investor updates and analyses, adding a human touch. Computer vision tracks engagement and emotion, allowing responsive website experiences.

As blockchain, the Internet of Things, 5G, and quantum computing emerge, finance will undergo seismic shifts. Smart contracts built on code logic will orchestrate complex deals at unprecedented speeds and volumes. AI will continue injecting intelligence across financial spheres, driving precision, personalization, and productivity. and transparency, redefining trust in the digital age. Augmented data analytics, courtesy of AI, are unveiling patterns and opportunities once shrouded in the vastness of market data, beyond the ken of human cognition.

AI in Healthcare

In healthcare, AI has become a vital partner - accelerating drug creation, honing diagnostic accuracy, enabling personalized medicine, and freeing staff from clerical tasks. Yet making care affordable and accessible remains paramount.

AI's ability to synthesize global data promises new therapeutic insights, moving beyond clinical trials' limits and costs. This democratized data could enable earlier interventions and reduced mortality if deployed ethically.

Telehealth, enhanced by AI's visual and linguistic skills, expands care's reach by simulated in-person consultations digitally. For practitioners, AI lifts the burden of administrative charting, returning precious time to cultivate human connections essential to healing. By automating the routine, AI restores focus on the empathy, touch, and presence at the heart of compassionate care.

AI in Education

In education, AI offers tools like writing assistants, quiz bots, and personalized tutoring to match each student's needs and gaps. Generative models now create lesson plans and curate content, inspiring teachers to adapt. Immersive virtual environments break down barriers, simulating costly real-world experiences for courtroom litigation, scientific experiments, and more.

AI also lightens institutions' administrative loads - automating admissions, records, billing, and scheduling. This frees staff to focus on teaching innovation, crucial for remote learning. Even test monitoring is now computerized for integrity.

For teachers, speech recognition translates verbal feedback into efficient written evaluations. Computer vision tracks student engagement, so instructors can adapt teaching methods in real-time and ensure no one is left behind. As education moves into the digital age, AI will continue serving as both a teaching aid and administrative ally.

The Democratizing Force

Here is my attempt to simplify the text in an inspiring tone while keeping a similar word count:

Far from the job-stealing threat it's made out to be, AI can democratize wisdom and unite privilege with promise. It spreads specialized insight and opens doors to opportunities that once felt exclusive – especially when directed with care.

As the past shows, with each technology boost comes a lift for humanity. Guided right, AI can stretch the creative reach of trailblazers, grow professional horizons for employees, and steer work to places where human brilliance rules — areas like strategy, innovation, and customer connections that stay resilient to automation.

Rather than replace us, envision how this supernova force could amplify our talents. See how its supercharged skills could collaborate with ours, fusing machine potential with human genius to illuminate new breakthroughs.

As AI changes rapidly, we gain more confidence that we can steer it. We can guide this tech toward a future of fairness, health, and meaningful jobs - not leave our fate to cold computer algorithms.

With every period of change, the demand for new skills arises. Change demands we learn new skills. Therefore, the outlook is hopeful, as we reset how we see tech - not as a taker of jobs but as a tool to lift human potential. Like old workhorses, AI, if we lead with ethics, can do tiring tasks that allow us to thrive as a human collective.

7 AI's Impact on Creative Industries

The integration of AI in creative industries has ushered in a new era of innovation, efficiency, and personalized experiences. AI is being leveraged to automate repetitive tasks, personalize creative output, and drive innovation across diverse creative domains such as art, music, film, fashion, and design. By analyzing large volumes of data, AI can personalize creative output for individual consumers, enhance productivity, and contribute to improved creativity and innovation. However, the adoption of AI in creative industries also raises ethical considerations, including the potential loss of human creativity and emotional intelligence.

The Role of AI in Unleashing Creativity

AI serves as a catalyst for unleashing creativity, offering new tools and methodologies that expand the horizons of artistic expression and entrepreneurial innovation. Through AI story generators, music composition algorithms, and visual art creation platforms, creatives are empowered to explore new frontiers of expression and ideation. The fusion of human ingenuity with AI's computational abilities has unlocked new possibilities for creative exploration, enabling creatives to push beyond traditional boundaries and embrace uncharted territories of expression.

The transformative potential of AI in creative industries is exemplified by the emergence of AI artists and innovative startups that have harnessed AI to automate repetitive tasks and create products with unprecedented efficiency and complexity. While the role of AI in creative industries is a subject of conflicting views, with some perceiving it as a threat to human creativity and employment, others recognize its potential to inspire and democratize creative expression.

What about Generative AI?

"Generative AI is the most powerful tool for creativity that has ever been created. It has the potential to unleash a new era of human innovation." - Elon Musk

Generative AI, a subfield of AI, is particularly awe-inspiring with its capacity to create new content, be it text, images, or other media forms. This capability unlocks a plethora of possibilities, from solving complex global issues to enhancing creativity and innovation. As we delve into the minds of AI experts and their generative AI quotes, their insights unveil the robust potential and the vast horizon that generative AI promises. Your text is accurate, but I'd like to rephrase it for clarity and readability:

Oriol Vinyals, a Research Scientist at Google, highlights the groundbreaking potential of generative models to revolutionize various industries. Due to rapid advancements in generative models, he notes that generative AI has a profound impact on machine intelligence, creativity, and industrial transformation, causing a fundamental change in how we perceive machine intelligence and creativity.

AI technology can significantly aid creatives in various ways. It can be used to generate new and inspiring ideas, assist in the creation of art and music, and even help in the development of innovative designs. Generative AI has the potential to push the boundaries of human creativity and open up new possibilities for artists, designers, and other creative professionals.

Furthermore, AI can be a valuable tool for creatives in terms of content creation and curation. It can help automate repetitive tasks, allowing creatives to focus more on the actual creative work. For example, AI-powered tools can be used to generate and optimize content for social media, assist in video and photo editing, and even help in writing and editing written content. This can ultimately save time and effort for creatives, enabling them to channel their energy into more meaningful and innovative pursuits.

In addition, AI can also play a significant role in personalizing the creative experience for both creators and consumers. By analyzing data and user behavior, AI can help tailor creative content to specific audiences, leading to more engaging and relevant experiences. This level of personalization can be particularly valuable in fields such as marketing, advertising, and entertainment, where reaching and resonating with the right audience is crucial.

The potential of AI to assist and enhance the work of creatives is vast and promising. From generating new ideas to automating repetitive tasks and personalizing creative experiences, AI has the power to revolutionize the creative process and enable new forms of expression. For those new to AI, understanding critical foundational knowledge helps demystify these powerful tools, bringing to light novel pathways for integration while avoiding potential perils. Just like attentive jockeys carefully direct their horses – applying wisdom, willpower, and skill to operate vehicles of much greater strength – by understanding essential concepts, everyday people gain the capacity for steering AI's incredible momentum toward positive progress rather than giving up one's direction to uncontrolled forces beyond their control.

8 AI Opportunities in Visual Arts and Design

AI in Visual Arts and Fashion Design

Artificial intelligence (AI has significantly impacted the visual arts and design, offering a wide array of capabilities that have revolutionized the creative process. AI's role in these industries is multifaceted, encompassing areas such as image generation, design optimization, and personalized user experiences.

For instance, AI has been increasingly utilized to create visually stunning and emotionally resonant images that align perfectly with a specific brief's look and feel. This has significant implications for the fashion industry, where AI is set to revolutionize the way brands create products and interact with customers.

For example, Runway ML offers a wide range of tools and models that can be used to generate images, videos, and interactive experiences, providing artists with new possibilities for creative expression. These tools allow for the generation of unique patterns and designs that can be seamlessly integrated into various products.

Generative AI tools such as these have become instrumental in creating unique designs and patterns. For instance, generative AI can be used in interior design and architecture to generate new ideas for room layouts, furniture placement, and color schemes.

Here are some fashion companies and organizations using AI in visual art and design:

1. **Mmerch**: Mmerch is a new fashion brand that is rethinking production using AI. The company allows customers to use text-to-image tools to mock up and purchase pieces with custom artwork. Mmerch offers limited-edition drops with unique, one-of-one clothing items designed using generative algorithms and linked to NFTs. The brand aims to combine AI and Web3 to serve as a new model for the industry, offering a new approach to fashion design and production.

2. **Cala**: Cala was the first fashion company to get early access to OpenAI's text-to-image product DALL-E. The company used generative AI design to guide designs for New York Fashion Week, showcasing the potential of AI in revolutionizing the fashion industry.

3. **Collina Strada**: Collina Strada used generative AI to demonstrate the creative possibilities of AI in fashion design and production.
4. **Revolve**: Revolve was a partner in AI Fashion Week to source generative AI design talent, showcasing the company's commit- ment to leveraging AI in fashion design and production.
5. **H&M Group**: H&M Group is introducing a generative AI design tool to its Creator Studio, demonstrating the company's investment in AI-powered design solutions and its commitment to staying ahead in the industry.
6. **Zara, H&M, Dior, Macy's, Nike, Valentino, Moncler, G-Star Raw, Levi's, Zegna, Kering, Gucci, and Prada**: These brands have all used AI in their business models, whether through AI chatbots, personalization, or trend forecasting. They have been at the forefront of leveraging AI to enhance customer engagement, boost sales, and stay relevant in a crowded market.

Furthermore, generative AI tools can be used to create personalized web designs, color palettes, logos, and other design elements. They are particularly beneficial for social media content creation and graphic design, allowing brands to create visually appealing and unique content for their customers. Additionally, these tools can be used to generate seamless patterns for various surfaces, offering a wide range of royalty-free patterns for products.

CASE STUDY

The 2018 auction of the AI-generated artwork "Portrait of Edmond de Belamy" by Obvious, a Paris-based art collective, for over $432,000 sent shockwaves through the art world. This landmark sale sparked a heated debate about the value of AI-generated art and challenged traditional notions of authorship, leading to increased interest in AI-generated art within the art market. The sale raised fundamental questions about the role of AI in the creative process and its potential to reshape the art world.

The use of AI in art creation has become a topic of significant interest and controversy. The "Portrait of Edmond de Belamy" was created using a Generative Adversarial Network (GAN), a type of machine learning model that can generate new content. This innovative approach to art creation has forced the art world to reconsider the definition of art and the role of human creativity in the context of AI-generated works.

The sale of AI-generated artwork at auction has prompted a re-evaluation of the relationship between human and machine creativity. It has also raised questions about the future of art and the potential for AI to influence and shape artistic expression. The impact of this sale has been felt across the art market, with gallerists, advisors, auction houses, and entrepreneurs grappling with the implications of AI in art creation and its influence on the traditional art market.

This case study has highlighted the transformative potential of AI in the visual arts, challenging established norms and sparking a broader conversation about the intersection of technology and creativity. The "Portrait of Edmond de Belamy" auction represents a pivotal moment in the history of art, signaling the emergence of AI as a significant force in the creative landscape.

The debate surrounding AI-generated art continues to evolve, with artists, scholars, and industry professionals exploring the implications of this groundbreaking development. The "Portrait of Edmond de Belamy" auction has set the stage for a new era in art, one that is defined by the dynamic interplay between human and machine creativity.

This case study underscores the need for ongoing dialogue and critical reflection on the role of AI in art and design, as well as its broader impact on society and culture. The "Portrait of Edmond de Belamy" auction has catalyzed innovation and introspection, challenging us to reconsider our assumptions about creativity, authorship, and the nature of artistic expression in the age of AI.

The sale of "Portrait of Edmond de Belamy" has demonstrated that AI-generated art has the potential to be both commercially successful and culturally significant. This case study has shed light on the complex and multifaceted relationship between AI and the visual arts, inspiring new perspectives, and insights into the future of creativity and innovation.

9 AI And Music

"Creativity is allowing yourself to make mistakes. Art is knowing which ones to keep." – SCOTT ADAMS

AI in Music and Sound: Transforming Creativity

Artificial Intelligence (AI) has significantly transformed the landscape of music and sound production, offering innovative solutions that have revolutionized the creative process. This chapter explores three key applications of AI in music and sound, showcasing the profound impact of AI-generated compositions and real-time music creation.

AI-Generated Music: Redefining Artistic Expression

AI algorithms have become adept at creating original compositions and generating music across various styles, from classical to contemporary. The emergence of AI in music composition has redefined the traditional creative process, offering new possibilities for artists and musicians. For instance, Aiva Technologies, an AI music composition company, provides a platform for creating and customizing original music. Their AI technology allows users to generate unique soundtracks tailored to their specific needs. The use of AI in music composition has sparked a broader conversation about the intersection of technology and creativity.

Music Recommendation: Enhancing the Creative Process

AI-powered systems have revolutionized the music recommendation process by suggesting musical elements, instrumentations, and arrangements to musicians and composers. For example, iZotope offers AI assistants for music production, providing tools that leverage machine learning to enhance the creative process for musicians and producers. This innovative approach has streamlined the music production process, offering valuable insights and skills for viewers to experiment with AI in their music.

Real-time Music Creation: Unleashing New Possibilities

Interactive AI systems enable real-time music improvisation, enhancing live performances and recordings. The integration of AI in real-time music creation has opened up new creative horizons, allowing musicians to experiment with different musical components like guitar solos and drumbeats. This transformative capability has redefined the dynamics of music creation, offering endless creative possibilities and helping musicians overcome creative blocks.

The rise of AI-generated music has led to companies and individuals offering unique takes on music creation. For instance, AI Music Studio is the first artificial intelligence startup that will revolutionize music production by making it accessible to millions of people. This groundbreaking development has forever changed the industry, inspiring new perspectives, and insights into the future of creativity and innovation.

The integration of AI in music and sound production has redefined the boundaries of creativity and innovation, offering new possibilities for artists, musicians, and producers. AI has become an indispensable tool for reshaping the future of artistic expression. As the industry continues to evolve, it is essential to embrace the transformative potential of AI in music and sound production, inspiring new forms of creativity and innovation.

This is a beginning look at the complex and multifaceted relationship between AI and the music industry, offering valuable insights into the future of creativity and innovation. As AI continues to advance, its role as a collaborative partner in the creative process will likely become even more pronounced, offering artists and creators unprecedented opportunities for innovation and artistic exploration.

CASE STUDY

The case study of Sony's Flow Machines developing the song "Daddy's Car," an AI-generated pop song in the style of The Beatles, represents a significant milestone in the integration of AI and music composition. This innovative achievement showcased AI's ability to compose music in the style of famous artists, marking a pivotal moment in the history of music creation. The impact of this development has been profound, demonstrating the potential for AI to assist composers and musicians in producing music in various genres and styles.

Sony's Flow Machines, through the creation of "Daddy's Car," exemplified the transformative potential of AI in music composition. By analyzing vast amounts of musical data, AI can adapt to real-time trending formats and provide relevant suggestions, offering valuable insights for artists and producers.

The "Daddy's Car" case study showcases the involved and multi-faceted relationship between AI and music composition, inspiring new perspectives, and insights into the future of creativity and innovation. As AI continues to advance, its role as a collaborative partner in the creative process will likely become even more pronounced, offering artists and creators unprecedented opportunities for innovation and artistic exploration.

This case study has underscored the need for ongoing dialogue and critical reflection on the role of AI in music composition, as well as its broader impact on society and culture. The "Daddy's Car" case study has served as a catalyst for innovation and introspection, challenging us to reconsider our assumptions about creativity, authorship, and the nature of artistic expression in the age of AI.

In conclusion, the "Daddy's Car" case study has demonstrated that AI-generated music has the potential to be both commercially successful and culturally significant. This groundbreaking development has forever changed the industry, inspiring new perspectives, and insights into a new era of digital and human collaborative creativity. As the industry continues to evolve, it is essential to embrace the transformative potential of AI in music composition, inspiring new forms of music.

10 AI And Writing

The future of creative writing is being reshaped by the integration of AI technology, offering a wide range of opportunities and challenges for writers and creators in the creative industries. AI is increasingly being used to develop higher-level thinking skills and encourage academic integrity in the classroom, providing strategies and examples for acknowledging and attributing AI-generated content ethically. Additionally, AI writers are being utilized as researchers to compile text for review, along with references for students to follow, informing original and carefully crafted work.

In the realm of AI writing tools, LogicBalls AI, Gimmefy, TexteroAI, and other specialty AI writing tools are gaining traction, offering a diverse range of features such as writing assistants, article summarizers, paraphrasing tools, and social media content generators.

These tools are designed to cater to various writing needs, from mainstream to obscure, and are being used to create auto-blogging websites or blogs for any niche. Furthermore, AI essay generators such as the one offered by CustomWritings.com are being used as personal writing assistants to craft impressive essays effortlessly.

However, it's important to note that while AI can analyze large datasets and identify patterns, it lacks the human experience and intuition needed to fully capture the nuances of human emotion. As a result, AI-generated writing can often feel mechanical or flat, lacking the depth and richness of human-created content.

The debate around AI's role in creative writing continues to be a topic of interest. While there are concerns regarding AI's potential to replace human creativity or lead to a loss of artistry, many view AI as a tool that can enhance the writing process. For instance, Jasper.ai is considered a cutting-edge AI writing assistant that can create original artwork based on text describing an image envisioned by the user. This harmonious blend of human imagination and AI-generated content is seen as a way to streamline the writing process and enhance creativity.

The Future of AI-Generated Storytelling

As AI continues to advance, its role in storytelling is expected to become even more pronounced, offering new possibilities for creative expression and innovation. In the realm of writing, AI- powered tools like Sudowrite and Simplified have emerged as powerful resources for writers, assisting in tasks such as creating story outlines, fleshing out chapters, and generating human-like text. These AI tools are designed to enhance creativity and increase writing efficiency, providing authors with a wealth of resources to streamline the writing process and bring their ideas to life. As one writer expressed, "It can be used for just about anything writing-related. Some artists, including writers, are using it to help them brainstorm ideas, outline their work, or even generate entire chapters or stories".

Several examples illustrate the transformative potential of artificial intelligence in the creative process. From AI-generated short stories and films to innovative AI writing tools, these examples showcase the evolving relationship between human creativity and AI-generated content.

As highlighted previously, Alasdair Mann is known as @Alementary on YouTube. He used AI to seek insights into potential challenges faced by the first space tourist, Dennis Tito. The AI-generated suggestions, combined with Mann's independent research, helped him craft a more captivating storyline, revealing AI's potential to enhance the creative process for writers.

In addition to these examples, several AI writing tools have gained popularity for their diverse capabilities. HyperWriteAI, for instance, is an AI writing tool that uses GPT technology to predict text, brainstorm new content, and edit content for tone and length. The tool has been used to create amusing and creative content, such as a Batman movie script with a creative twist and an award ceremony acceptance speech.

The Good AI is another notable example, offering an AI essay writer site that uses artificial intelligence to write essays in seconds. Users can provide a title, word count, and optional tone, and the AI generates the essay, illustrating how AI is being used to automate the writing process for various types of content.

These examples highlight the diverse and innovative applications of AI in writing, from generating compelling narratives to enhancing the creative process for writers. As AI continues to advance, its role in storytelling and content creation is expected to become even more noticeable, offering new opportunities for creative expression and innovation.

Part II:
Future of Fashion and the Creative Economy

11 Fashion and AI – A Strong Use Case of an Industry Benefiting from AI

In the rich tapestry of human endeavor, the threads of fashion and artificial intelligence (AI) are intertwining with increasing complexity and beauty. This fusion brings forth not just a transformation in how we clothe ourselves, but in how we conceive creativity and success in an age driven by technological marvels. Let's take a look at how the fashion industry is harnessing AI as a force for growth and innovation.

The Trillion Dollar Opportunity

The fashion industry, a vibrant and ever-evolving marketplace, has now collided with the formidable force of AI. This union is set to redefine the economic landscape. With the fashion market valued at $1.5 trillion (Forbes, 2022), and AI's expected growth to $1.4 trillion by 2029 (Fortune Business Insights, 2022), we stand at the precipice of a new era. The momentum of AI within fashion is poised for a staggering increase, with a projected growth to $4.4 billion by 2027, marking a rise of over 1600% from 2018 (AI Multiple, 2019). This unprecedented synergy promises to weave a new narrative of human-machine collaboration.

Algorithms: The Catalysts of Creative Abundance

AI was once feared as a threat to human creativity. Yet algorithms have become unexpected partners in the creative process. This fusion of human and machine reveals a deep pool of collective creativity. For example, Zalando's 'Project Muse' used AI to design 40,000 new fashion items. By studying past styles and trends, the algorithms crafted innovative looks (Zalando, 2022. This shows how AI can boost, not replace, the human artist.

Retail Reimagined

In the retail space, AI has reintroduced a sense of allure and connection that seemed lost to the digital revolution. Companies like StyleMe and AiFi are at the forefront of this renaissance, with technologies that restore the tactile joy of shopping and personalize retail environments to individual consumer behaviors (StyleMe, 2022; AiFi, 2022. AI here is not a replacement but a complement that enriches the retail experience.

Sustainable Fashion Through Intelligent Design

AI's role extends beyond consumerism into the heart of sustainability. By employing data analytics, the industry can significantly cut fabric waste, as noted by the Boston Consulting Group, which could prevent 20-50% of the waste traditionally produced by fashion houses (BCG, 2022). Platforms like Craftwork empower brands to bypass multiple physical sampling stages, opting instead for digital finalization of collections (Craftwork, 2022. With Queen of Raw's innovative apps, upcycling becomes not just a trend but a transformative movement in fashion (Queen of Raw, 2022.

AI's Leaders in Fashion

The avant-garde of this movement consists of companies like Stitch Fix, which pairs personal stylists with AI to curate custom wardrobes (Stitch Fix, 2022), and ThredUp), which uses machine learning for precise pricing of secondhand apparel (ThredUp, 2022. These pioneers represent the dawning of a new paradigm where AI and human ingenuity coalesce to redefine the fashion landscape.

Envisioning an AI-Inclusive Future

We stand at a crossroads where the narrative of AI in fashion is ours to write. Rather than yielding to dystopian prophecies, we have the opportunity to sculpt a future where AI serves as an amplifier of human talent. We should be intentional about embedding our data and neural networks with the values that celebrate creativity, diversity, and sustainability. In this way, we can ensure that the future of fashion—and indeed, all industries—reflects our highest ideals and aspirations.

Key Companies Propelling Fashion Forward with AI

Each of these companies exemplifies AI's transformative potential within the fashion industry:

1. **Zalando** – Their generative design algorithm 'Project Muse' is not just a design tool; it's a testament to AI's role as a collaborator in creativity.
2. **Stitch Fix** – Merges the intuition of stylists with AI's analytical power, delivering personalized fashion at scale.
3. **ThredUp** – Uses AI to redefine the resale space, proving that sustainability and technology are a match made in sartorial heaven.
4. **AiFi** – Their AI-infused sensors are redefining the retail experience, making shopping seamless and intuitive.
5. **Ayyay** – Illustrates how AI can solve the age-old issue of fit, merging technology with tailor-made precision.
6. **Farfetch** – Showcases AI's knack for customer service, enhancing the online shopping journey with smart recommendations.
7. **ModeSens** – Uses AI to navigate the vast sea of online retail, ensuring consumers get the best deals and selections.
8. **Heuritech** – Their trend forecasting capabilities are like a crystal ball powered by AI, helping brands stay ahead of the curve.
9. Aesthetic Integration – Merges the art of design with the science of AI, opening doors to new realms of fashion creativity.
10. **InvertUI** – Their virtual fitting room technology is redefining the try-before-you-buy experience, all thanks to AI.

Additional Use Cases Spanning Design, Retail, and Sustainability

AI's application in fashion isn't just revolutionary; it's varied and vast, touching every aspect of the industry:

- **Supply Chain Coordination** – AI streamlines production, ensuring ethical practices are at the forefront.
- **Material Matching Algorithms** – These tools reduce waste by optimizing fabric selection, a win for both designers and the planet.
- **Blockchain Traceability** – Offers a transparent view into the sourcing of materials, bolstering ethical consumption.
- **Upcycling Apps** – AI breathes new life into deadstock, turning waste into wanted wear.
- **Voice Command Assistants** – They're not just for smartphones; AI aids shoppers in making informed style choices.

- **Augmented Reality Try-Ons** – Brings the dressing room to your living room, thanks to AI.
- **Generative Design Algorithms** – Expand creative output, pushing the boundaries of what's possible in fashion design.

The Industry's Uncertain Yet Hopeful AI Future

As we stand at the crossroads of innovation, AI isn't a harbinger of obsolescence for human designers; it's the dawn of a new era where tech and talent synergize. We are at the helm, guiding AI not toward cold automation but toward a future where technology and human values coexist, enriching our culture and crafting a narrative of inclusivity, diversity, and sustainability. This is where artists and technologists come together, cultivating innovation that also contributes positively to humanity.

This is the exciting beginning of fashion's renaissance, with AI at the forefront and human creativity as its guide. Together, we can craft a future where fashion isn't just about the clothes we wear but the values we embody and share with each new moment in time.

12 AI, Web3 and Fashion

In our journey similar to "The Jockey on the Horse," where navigating the unpredictable is part of the thrill, we find ourselves at a crossroads where artificial intelligence (AI and Web3 aren't just accessories to the fashion world but integral threads in its evolving tapestry.

AI + Fashion + The Future of the Internet

AI in fashion has spread its wings far beyond the confines of design and sustainability. It's pioneering a new frontier where the intimacy of personalized styling and the foresight of predictive design become entangled with machine learning and data analytics.

Creative Personalized Styling

In the fashion landscape, startups are blending the nuanced eye of a human stylist with the scalable precision of algorithms to create looks that resonate with individual tastes. Stitch Fix, a leader in this hybrid approach, marries data-driven suggestions with human oversight, ensuring each curated box is a tailored extension of the customer's unique style profile.

As AI's palate for personalization grows richer, it will serve as the initial integrator, pulling together suggestions based on style quizzes, while the human stylist's touch will refine the final garment selections. This partnership between man and machine aims to partner the best of both worlds into the framework of fashion retail.

Predictive Design Based on Market or Sales Data

Moving upstream in the creative process, AI's potential to mitigate the risks of speculative design is immense. By swiftly steering through vast pools of market data, generative algorithms are becoming the new oracles of fashion, forecasting the rise and fall of trends with a precision that was once the realm of intuition and experience.

For instance, Heuritech's digital gaze extends across social media, identifying the nascent ripples of tomorrow's fashion waves. With predictive analytics growing more acute, these insights can level the playing field, offering small and independent brands the same visionary foresight that once only behemoths of the industry could wield.

Immersive Augmented or Virtual Experiences

Beyond virtual try-ons, the fashion world is on the brink of an AR/VR renaissance, with companies like Obsess crafting immersive digital showrooms that transport customers beyond the confines of their homes to virtual spaces of splendor and style.

Imagine selecting an outfit and seeing your avatar model it against the backdrop of a virtual Roman holiday. As the metaverse beckons, the confluence of AI-driven design and immersive realities is set to revolutionize the runway, rendering borders and boundaries obsolete.

Supply Chain Visibility and Optimization

AI's lens also brings into focus the often-murky waters of the supply chain. Startups like LinkSights are employing AI to shed light on the once not-so-transparent channels of apparel production, ensuring that brands can account for every stitch and seam from cotton field to storefront.

Platforms like Sourcemap, birthed from the minds at MIT, offer interactive mappings that paint a complete picture of a brand's environmental impact, pinpointing opportunities for significant sustainability enhancements throughout the supply chain.

Optimizing Production with Digital Twins

In the factories, the dawn of "digital twins" is revolutionizing prototyping. CLO 3D as well as Browzwear's suite of tools, allows for the digital iteration of garments, simulating everything from stitch to fabric behavior, reducing the need for physical samples and accelerating the journey from concept to consumer.

Emerging Startups Propelling Fashion Forward

At the forefront of this revolution are startups that fuse technical expertise with aesthetic acumen, crafting AI that can generate complete 3D garment designs and offering sensory-rich retail experiences that redefine the shopping journey.

From Unspun's on-demand fit customization, harnessing body scanning for jeans that mirror every curve, to the Sixth Sense's augmented physical retail spaces, the startups of today are the leaders of a fashion future where creativity and technology moves hand in hand.

In the AI-infused era of fashion, our creative outlook should not be hindered by fear but rather highlight the potential of harmony and innovation. As we embrace these new tools, let's also bring to life a future where every detail is informed by ethical practice and every fabric tells a story of sustainable progress. With courage and foresight, we can write this new chapter where the synergy of AI and human creativity dresses the world not just in clothes, but in the very dreams of what fashion can become.

13 The Web3 Connection – A Deeper Dive with Fashion as a Use Case

In the realm of innovation, as in fashion, each new trend is a tribute to the legacy of its predecessors. The inception of Web3 is akin to a new phase of the internet, promising autonomy, and individual empowerment, mirroring the transformative effects AI has had on design and creativity.

An Evolving Internet: From Commerce to Empowerment
Web 1.0 served as the foundation of the modern web, the first to bring connectivity that would eventually blanket the globe. It was the birth of commerce in cyberspace, a bazaar of static pages similar to the early markets of civilization. Then came Web 2.0, the social revolution, interconnectivity where the user could contribute to the grand design. But this era, for all its shared inventiveness, also carried a hidden pattern of surveillance and control, where our personal data was pulled by unseen algorithms.

Web3: A Promise of Decentralization
Web3 heralds a return to the original intent of the web—an opportunity where each user controls their data. Blockchain technology, with its decentralized ledger, is the shuttle that passes back and forth, ensuring that each data point is secure, and each creation is true to its creator.

Blockchain and Cryptocurrency: A New Currency for Creativity
The blockchain is a new platform for fashion's digital era, promising a world where designs and transactions are moved directly between creator and consumer. Cryptocurrencies, as vibrant and varied as fabrics, offer a means of exchange free from the constraints of traditional economic systems, to ignite a regeneration in fashion.

Decentralized Autonomous Organizations (DAOs): Weaving Together a New Governance

DAOs offer a fresh take on organizational structures. Imagine a fashion house where every tailor, apprentice, and artist have a say in the design and direction of the atelier. DAOs propose such a world, where smart contracts bring together the collective will of a distributed community, crafting a picture of cooperation and shared vision.

Metaverse: The New Frontier of Fashion

Envision the metaverse as the new fashion runway, a boundless virtual space where creativity is only limited by imagination. Brands can showcase their designs in a world unbound by physics, allowing for an interplay of artistry and technology that stretches the imagination.

Real-World Examples: The Connection of Web3 and AI

We are already witnessing the integration of AI with Web3 principles in projects like The Fabricant, a digital fashion house that creates clothing that exists only in the virtual world, sewn together with the virtual threads and secured through blockchain technology.

Sustainability and Ethical Considerations: The Conscious Cloth of Web3

As we create new digital wardrobes, we must prioritize ethics and eco practices. Projects like Provenance, which uses blockchain to verify the authenticity and ethical sourcing of materials, show us a future where the clothes we wear—both digital and physical—are made in a way that honors the earth and its inhabitants.

The Future We Create Together

Just as the Jockey on the Horse must work in harmony to achieve victory, so must we align with Web3 to move closer to a future that empowers the individual. This chapter is a call to intentionally create a picture of the future that embodies rich culture, diversity, and the human touch, to ensure that the digital future is a balanced future where humanity comes first.

In the world of Web3, we are all participants in the digital era, and what we create will define the future of connectivity, creativity, and commerce. As we find our way through the complexities of this emerging technology, let's remember the lessons of the past and take the best of and bring it into the future, developing a digital Renaissance that honors the individual as the master of their creation.

JOCKEY ON THE HORSE

14 Shaping Fashion's Future - Blending My Designs with New Tech

"Style is a reflection of your attitude and your personality," Shawn Ashmore once said, a sentiment that has resonated with me from my first forays into the world of design to my current role as a pioneer at the intersection of fashion and technology. It's a journey that began not with the intention to follow well-trodden paths, but to chart a new course – one where my unique vision as a designer could harmonize with the innovative cadences of emerging tech.

Amplifying My Creative Gifts

Long before AI became my collaborator, psychology has always been my partner in creating designs, stories, and products, that offer insights into the human psyche while promising avenues to foster well-being. Along the journey of designer turned author turned technology junky, there has always been the desire to use my creative gifts to inspire others. Incorporating technology into my life as a tool for creativity, efficiency, and distribution has allowed me to increase the positive impact I want to make on the world.

I was born in Jamaica and one of six children. I was the first generation to attend college in the US and throughout high school leaned into my desire to become a doctor to help others like me, live their happiest lives. Although the method of how I am pursuing my purpose has changed, the desire to help and inspire hasn't. It was fashion that became my NorthStar to accomplish this goal, and thus expanded into speaking, writing, podcasting, and production.

It was technology that continuously helped me along the way, find new means of easily creating and sharing what I produced.

From Concept to Couture: The AI Collaboration

The evolution from psychologist to fashion innovator was not just a change in profession but a fusion of disciplines. As a high-end designer, my creations are not only born from the inspiration around me but are brought to life with the aid of tools such as Generative AI. As a creative, it is exciting to see how technology can be a great equalizer and a means of opportunity and access.

Although I was trained in traditional fashion design, I incorporate data-driven insights to enhance my work and generative AI algorithmic magic to craft pieces that resonate with contemporary desires while retaining the timeless elegance of haute couture. It's an approach that marries Coco Chanel's mandate for uniqueness with the inexorable march of technological progress.

AI as the Evidence of the Modern Era

The loom, once the cornerstone of textile innovation, has now given way to digital fabrication methods, AI-driven trend forecasting, and virtual fittings. These tools do not diminish the designer's role but augment it, allowing us to craft experiences and garments that were once the realm of fantasy.

For instance, AI's capacity to simulate draping and material behavior before a single thread is woven, challenges the very notion of trial and error, allowing designers to envision the end before the beginning. It's a powerful ally in a designer's quest for perfection, ensuring that the leap from the mind's eye to the mannequin is both bold and precise.

A Future Steeped with Ethics and Aesthetics

As we look toward the future, it's clear that AI will increasingly inform the way we create, consume, and contemplate fashion.

However, as this technology plays a stronger role within the industry, it is imperative that we remain the ethical masters of the technology. We must ensure that the values of sustainability, ethical production, and inclusive beauty are the patterns that AI helps us replicate and enhance.

Designing the Future

My journey from aspiring doctor to couture fashion designer is a testament to the power of listening to one's inner voice and the courage to embrace change. It is also a narrative that underscores the transformative potential of AI when it is guided by human creativity, insight, and ethical consideration.

In this chapter, we will delve deeper into the symbiotic relationship between the visionary designer and the digital tools that are reshaping the fashion industry. We'll explore how, together, we can stitch a future that honors both the legacy of haute couture and the innovative spirit that drives us toward tomorrow.

Generative AI: The New Muse in Fashion

Generative AI is rapidly becoming the vanguard of creativity in fashion, serving as a new muse for designers. It's not just a tool; it's a collaborative partner offering a fresh palette of possibilities. With its ability to learn from existing data and generate new content, generative AI is a digital loom weaving together the past and the present to create novel future trends.

Generative AI Tools for Fashion Designers and Creatives

Today, designers have an array of generative AI tools at their fingertips. Programs like Google's DeepDream and NVIDIA's StyleGAN have revolutionized the creative process. These tools allow designers to input their sketches and ideas, which the AI then uses to generate countless iterations, offering new combinations and inspirations that might never have been conceived by the human mind alone.

Impacting Fashion Design and Creativity Industry

Generative AI is transforming the fashion industry at every level. In fashion design, it's being used to create intricate patterns and textures that challenge our notion of what's possible. For fashion campaigns, AI-generated models and scenes provide cost-effective and diverse visual content. In fashion photography, AI algorithms are used to enhance images, creating perfect lighting and mood that align with campaign themes. The creativity industry, as a whole, is witnessing a paradigm shift where AI-generated content is becoming indistinguishable from human-made, challenging the traditional boundaries of artistry and authorship.

A 2021 report from McKinsey & Company highlights that about 9% of the fashion sector has begun experimenting with generative AI, indicating the nascent stage of this technology's integration into the industry. However, the same report projects a rapid increase in adoption over the next five years, driven by the demand for personalized and sustainable fashion solutions.

The Evolution of Generative AI

The future of generative AI in fashion is bright and brimming with potential. As machine learning algorithms become more sophisticated, we can expect AI to provide increasingly nuanced designs that are tailored to individual styles and preferences. The ability to generate sustainable and zero-waste patterns is another frontier that generative AI is poised to conquer, as predicted by a study from the University of California, Berkeley.

Getting Started with Generative AI

For those eager to ride the wave of generative AI, getting started is less about acquiring a new set of skills and more about embracing a new creative process.

Begin by exploring platforms like MidJourney, Leonardo AI, and Runway ML, which offer an accessible interface for experimenting with generative models without the need for extensive coding knowledge.

Upskilling with Generative AI

To truly harness the power of generative AI, designers and creatives must upskill. This involves not only learning how to use generative tools but also understanding the principles of machine learning that drive them. Online courses from institutions like Coursera and edX provide pathways for those looking to deepen their understanding of AI and apply it to their creative endeavors. These cover a range of topics, including:

- The application of generative models in textile design, pattern making, and garment construction
- The use of AI for sustainable fashion design, such as predicting trends and reducing waste
- The art of prompt engineering for fashion-focused AI models
- The ethics of AI-generated fashion content and how to navigate issues of authorship and ownership

By upskilling with generative AI, fashion creatives can:

- Develop a critical understanding of how AI models can enhance their design process and workflow

- Learn how to use AI as a tool for research and inspiration, rather than just a means of automation
- Explore the frontiers of human-AI collaboration and co-creation in fashion

Part III:
Career Transitions, Mastering Change, and Creating Growth

15 Job Jitters – Navigating Career Changes in the AI Era

As we stand on the cliff of this new century, it's as if we've been cast into the future without a script, drifting aimlessly in a sea where change is the only constant. In this change, we will see new and old roles come and go. Some we can predict, many we can't. Within this moment of uncertainty is an opportunity to create new ways of carrying out these roles, ways that will give back more time to spend on the things we love and with those we love.

We are in an era where artificial intelligence (AI and automation are reshaping the workforce, kindling both concern and exhilaration. And yet, it's precisely this intersection of innovation and humanity that calls for a dance of wisdom and adaptability, where transitions become opportunities for growth and enrichment. In this fluid land- scape, understanding the shifting dynamics involving our career pathways highlights the way forward. Here, we explore the transformative impact of AI on employment, delineating the roles that may fade and those that will thrive, as well as the emergence of novel vocations in this new digital age.

AI and the Future of Jobs: A Statistical Viewpoint

1. By 2025, AI and automation are poised to displace 85 million jobs, marking a significant pivot in the global job market (World Economic Forum).
2. An expansive view by McKinsey suggests that up to 800 million global workers could be displaced by automation come 2030.
3. Amidst the ebb of certain professions, AI simultaneously heralds the genesis of 97 million new roles by 2025, crafting a rebalanced job landscape (World Economic Forum).

Navigating the Shift: Which Jobs Are on the Edge of Extinction

Most at-risk jobs:

Data entry clerks and administrative assistants find themselves on the cusp of automation, alongside accountants and assembly line workers. Retail roles, including cashiers and telemarketers, as well as service positions like fast food workers, are also navigating this new terrain (Forbes).

Least at-Risk Jobs:
Conversely, the human touch remains irreplaceable in nursing, medicine, dentistry, and veterinary care. Engineers, educators, managers, cybersecurity mavens, AI specialists, and creatives – from musicians to designers – continue to carve indispensable niches (McKinsey, Business Insider).

The Wake of New Professions:
EMERGENT ROLES

- **AI Trainers**: Custodians of knowledge, these professionals feed vast datasets into burgeoning AI systems, shaping their learning.
- **Explainers**: Interpreters of the opaque, they demystify the inner workings of machine learning, rendering the complex comprehensible.
- **AI Ethicists**: Champions of values, they weave the fabric of ethical codes into the digital framework, ensuring AI aligns with humanistic principles.
- **Conversational Interface Designers**: Artisans of interaction, crafting seamless, intuitive dialogues with chatbots.
- **Avatar Programmers**: Sculptors of the virtual self, they breathe life into digital personae, crafting nuanced identities.
- **Automation Consultants**: Advisors on the confluence of innovation, guiding the integration of smart technologies into the fabric of business.
- **Augmented Reality Architects**: Visionaries of immersive experiences, they paint new worlds over the canvas of our reality.
- **Quantum Machine Learning Experts**: Alchemists of algorithms, they harness the enigmatic powers of quantum computing to forge new frontiers in AI.

As we move forward on this unscripted journey into the AI Age, it's not the speed of change but the direction we steer the horse. In the synergy of humans and machines, we find not an end but a new beginning, an invitation to reimagine the essence of work, value, and purpose.

Job Forecasts in Flux

As we navigate the tides of change, news headlines often paint a pessimistic picture of a future where automation threatens the workforce. With predictions that a significant fraction of roles may disappear and be reimagined due automation within a decade, it's essential to unpack these forecasts with a discerning eye.

According to Pricewaterhouse Coopers (PwC) analysis, in 2018 titled "Will Robots Really Take Our Jobs?" they provide a nuanced viewpoint; "By the 2030s, up to 30% of jobs in the UK could be vulnerable to automation. This doesn't mean that one out of every three jobs will be automated but that they involve tasks that could potentially be automated. Additionally, the rise of automation technologies will create demands for labor."

The changing landscape signifies transformation rather than extinction, where new opportunities emerge to counterbalance the decline of ones. The digital era has ushered in industries that previous generations could hardly have envisioned. Societies shape their futures by blending beliefs, policy implementations and paths leading toward horizons. These results can thrive through an approach, to innovation or deteriorate without guidance.

Embracing AI: Upskilling and Adapting

In the face of these shifts staying idle is not an option. To fully embrace this era, we need to embody flexibility and foresight. Companies that support training programs promote learning opportunities. Offer aid, for educational endeavors demonstrate a commitment to developing the adaptability of their workforce.

However, the process of adjusting goes beyond acquiring skills. It involves nurturing a growth-oriented mindset that embraces the evolving dynamics of today's workplace. In a time where careers transition between freelance roles the resilience once associated with entrepreneurs becomes essential for everyone. Prioritizing skills centered on interaction creative thinking and strategic planning ensures a workforce to complement rather than compete with AI capabilities.

Currently, AI excels in data analysis while human strengths lie in building relationships fostering creativity and making nuanced decisions. Grounding our advancement in enduring values like courage, wisdom. and promoting good is essential, for our progress.

It's important to make sure that our commitment to innovation doesn't overshadow the core values that support us. Finding this balance is key to navigating the era of intelligence shaping a future that respects tradition while boldly embracing the new.

Emerging Roles in the AI Economy

In the swiftly unfolding evolution of AI, each thread of advancement opens opportunities for the agile learner. An industry forecast speculates the need for over 4 million specialists in key AI domains in the near future, spanning roles from data scientists to machine learning engineers, AI security analysts to robotics programmers, and AR/VR developers, among others (Qiang, 2022). Beyond these, new professions emerge at the confluence of human creativity and algorithmic precision, crafting solutions once deemed unattainable in domains as diverse as healthcare, sustainability, and education.

The approach to technology's growing role must evolve from competition to collaboration, strengthening our collective capabilities through human-AI partnerships.

This synergistic balance between human and computer sets off a multiplier effect, where computational power is harmonized with the irreplaceable life experience of the human spirit—something a machine cannot do on its own. Although the future may seem filled with fear of the unknown, with an intentional focus on the wellbeing of humans, our anxiety turns to assurance of progress and growth.

The AI Job Elimination Fears – Justified or Not?

In the past, the persistent narrative about technology and innovation is a direct cause of widespread job loss always stood challenged the statistical evidence that shows a different outcome. Consider the advent of the ATM; initial fears prophesied the end of bank tellers. As time went on, we saw that their introduction saw teller jobs double as ATMs facilitated a boom in customer service demand, necessitating more human staff to manage complex sales and service interactions beyond the machine's capability (Bessen, 2015).

At the moment, while algorithms master the realm of calculation, the uniquely human faculties—complex communication, creative problem-solving, and deep relational understanding—remain securely in human hands for the foreseeable future. If as a collective, we continue to fixate on a more dystopian, unhappy ending, will we prevent the collective will to prepare for a future where technology and humanity advance together?

When we steer the horse towards virtues that align with humans thriving and living with equity, justice, compassion, and liberty—we unlock new realms of potential. It is by elevating these principles above all else that we chart a course of progress, not by sheer computational power, but by the values we hold sacred. Let's sprint forward, unmoved by fear, towards a horizon rich with promise and shared prosperity.

Bridging Job Disruption with New Assistants

The march of progress has always brought with it, tools that alleviate the burdens of work, transforming challenges into opportunities. Just as spreadsheets once revolutionized the way we manage data, today's AI-driven assistants are redefining productivity in the workplace.

Consider Fireflies, a pioneering platform offering an AI assistant adept at joining virtual meetings to not only transcribe discussions but also highlight key points and nudge us with follow-up tasks. This innovation ensures that the momentum from our meetings translates into tangible outcomes.

The introduction of such technology means that the essential, yet often tedious, task of documentation evolves from a manual to an automated process, freeing up human intellect for tasks that demand a personal touch. With the capability to search transcripts by keyword, we're now empowered with a memory aid that surpasses the limits of our natural recall. The result is a workplace where the minutiae of minute-taking give way to action-driven collaboration.

Yet, wisdom in the use of these tools is paramount. It's vital to strike a balance, ensuring these digital assistants complement rather than replace human oversight, especially given their occasional lapses in accuracy. When used judiciously, they promise to relieve us of mundane tasks, redirecting our focus to where it matters most.

Implications for the Future of Work

As we take a look into the future of work, it's clear that technologies like AI note-taking point to a day when machines might surpass human capacity in certain cognitive functions. However, the typical human domains of empathy, nuanced communication, and creative innovation remain uniquely ours, less susceptible to the infringement of automation.

Despite fears of job loss, history tells us that with every technological upheaval, new paths of employment and progress open up. To harness this potential, we must recalibrate our economic structures, envisioning corporations as entities responsible not just for profit but for the well-being of the planet and the stability of their workforce.

In recognizing the value of both the digital tools at our disposal and the human colleagues beside us, we can maintain a dynamic, forward-thinking approach. It's a journey that calls for agility, positivity, and a focus on solutions. With a steadfast commitment to principles of justice and equity, we unlock a future where automation serves as a liberator, not a suppressor, of human potential.

Jobs and Automation: A Detailed Look

Communications Industry

- Public Relations Specialists: With a low probability of automation, these professionals' ability to respond with sensitivity to crises remains distinctly human.
- Editors: While AI can streamline proofreading, the strategic guidance of manuscripts still demands a human touch.

Film/TV Industry

- Actors: Their irreplaceable emotional expression and individual creativity keep them safe from automation.
- Producers & Directors: The intricate art of storytelling and project management is a bastion of human ingenuity.

- Camera Operators: There's an increasing likelihood of automation in filming, but the artistry of cinematography remains a human endeavor.

Food & Hospitality
- Restaurant Cooks: The rise of robotic kitchens presents a tangible threat, yet the culinary arts' human element endures.
- Waitstaff: Though under threat from automation, the essence of hospitality is human connection.
- Hotel Receptionists: AI can field inquiries, but the warmth of a human welcome remains unmatched.

Writing Industry
- Technical Writers: Machine learning is making strides, but the final quality checks necessitate human expertise.
- Creative Writers: The depth of human imagination and storytelling cannot be replicated by algorithms, keeping this realm securely human for now.

16 Managing Change, Uncertainty and Anxiety

"We can't solve problems by using the same kind of thinking we used when we created them." - ALBERT EINSTEIN

Developing Adaptability and Resilience

The sheer pace of technological change today can feel dizzying. Futurist Thomas Frey predicts that "over the next 10 years we'll experience more transformations than we've seen in the past 250 years." Oxford scholars estimate automation alone will transform over 70 million jobs in the next decade (Nedelkoska & Quintini, 2018).

Navigating such mounting volatility understandably fuels unease. People are worried that AI and automation will disrupt job security and find it hard to imagine outcomes in the midst of times ahead. However, it's important to consider things from a different an angle. Throughout history every era has experienced changes that challenged established ways of life. Like the Industrial Revolution, the Digital Age and so on. During each of these periods those who resisted change were

left behind while those who adapted their skills and attitudes to match the evolving landscape discovered new possibilities.

As ecological philosopher Alan Watts noted, "The only way to make sense out of change is to plunge into it, move with it, and join the dance." The coming years will reward those most willing to skillfully adapt.

To build resilience we must first accept that constant change is now the standard. Fear arises when we hold onto fixed beliefs, about the future of adapting to situations. By releasing securities like "jobs, for life" we can focus on creating stronger internal foundations proactively.

Psychologist Madeline Levine highlights that children benefit hugely from learning adaptability versus fixating on particular career identities. This developmental alacrity will serve them well as AI restructures workplace needs. Levine asks, "How do we prepare kids both materially and emotionally so they are ready to explore careers and opportunities we can't yet imagine?" By concentrating less on hard skills and more on nurturing change-adept qualities like curiosity, creativity, critical reasoning, and connection to passions, young professionals gain autonomy to pivot roles fluidly as once-stable occupational maps get redrawn.

Cultivating Growth Mindset

Beyond developing individual readiness to move with the changing times, collective focus toward innovation opportunities rather than disruption threats, greatly influences societal outcomes.

Stanford psychologist Carol Dweck's research on mindset transformation reveals that environments encouraging a "growth mindset" - the belief abilities can be developed continuously through dedication - empower achievement, while fixed mindsets that label people according to limited snapshots of talent or potential, actually undermine success.

This insight has profound implications for AI-era education. Are students praised for being "smart" or for persevering? Are workers being re-skilled or simply relegated to the "unemployable" heap by corporate efficiency metrics? Media storylines and policy signals dramatically sway public attitudes and confidence.

Jacob Morgan's studies indicate that organizations and nations that openly discuss AI communicate goals effectively and continuously improve their workforce will excel in times of change. Those who view workers as tools than valued collaborators risk lowering morale, productivity and consumer trust.

Choosing career paths, over productivity gains is essential. It's crucial that our education systems encourage learning and that companies invest significantly in developing their employees. This shift, in mindset should become the norm embraced by society.

Managing Stress and Anxiety

Amidst the changes happening around us it's important to acknowledge and deal with the stress and anxiety that often come along. Whether it's following the guidance, from experts at the Mayo Clinic or embracing approaches, like Germany's "Work 4.0 " there are different ways we can adapt and succeed in times of change. Making lifestyle adjustments prioritizing well-being and planning ahead are all tools that can help us navigate through the psychological effects of a world shaped by AI.

For those feeling the weight of change most deeply, the art of de-cluttering—paring down life's complexities to the essentials—can be a great starting point. This act of simplification allows for the space to breathe, and to engage with life and career in ways that are proactive and creative, rather than reactive and confined.

An Invitation to the Signs of Change

As we stand on the precipice of this new age, we're faced with a profound choice. Will we recoil in fear at the unknowns, or will we step forward with courage, with the conviction that our collective mindset will shape the future?

We must remember that the future is not a distant reality—it is being written with each decision we make. Let's choose to approach this era of change as an era of opportunity, an invitation to dance with the unknown, to join in the co-creation of a world that honors our humanity amidst the march of machines.

17 Embracing the Uncertain Future

"The only thing that is constant is change," Heraclitus famously wrote, and his words resonate with greater truth in this era of surprising technological leaps. With artificial intelligence (AI and automation at the helm, the framework of our society is being remade at a pace once unimaginable. With super-fast transformation comes both excitement and hesitation —yet as I explored in "Unleash Your Supernova," it is in the heart of uncertainty that the seeds of what is possible are sewn.

In this chapter, we will journey through the art of resilience, drawing from my background as a psychologist and my intimate experience with change. Here, you will discover strategies to:

- Rethink and reshape beliefs about the nature of uncertainty.
- Deepen self-awareness to navigate change with intention and wisdom.
- Foster and fortify social ties to endure widespread disruption.

With courage, creativity, and compassion as our guideposts, let's step into technological progress, ready to play our part in its direction and story.

Rewriting Limiting Beliefs about Uncertainty

Feelings of uneasiness in the face of change, which may be frightening, are completely natural. However, we must remember that these feelings stem from speculation, not certainty. Stanford's Kelly McGonigal encourages a pivot from anxiety to anticipation, shifting our face-to-face encounter with the unknown from fear to joy.

Begin by scrutinizing your beliefs. Do you equate change with fear, the way turbulence might unsettle a flight's passenger? Remember, turbulence is not an indication of disaster but a natural occurrence. Growth, too, requires us to pass through areas of doubt to reach a new stability. Recollect instances when life's detours uncovered new paths. What did these moments teach you about uncertainty and opportunity?

Dr. Ron Friedman tells us that we thrive amid moderate uncertainty, where comfort meets the challenge. Introduce variability to your routine—take a new path, try a different coffee blend. These simple acts of diversification prepare your mind for more significant shifts, training you for the larger collective transformations ahead.

By challenging the story that casts change as a villain, we open ourselves to a new plot—one where technological advancement is perfectly set up for human advancement. Risks are inherent, but our shared will can steer this ship towards ethical and compassionate shores. What beliefs will empower you to face the future with optimism?

Cultivating Self-Knowledge to Respond Consciously

In the highest moments of uncertainty, our primal instincts often take the reins, bypassing the wisdom of intentional thought. Self-inquiry is the lighthouse in the dark, offering a brighter path in

how we can interact with change. It's about tuning in to the whispers of our body, the echoes of past experiences, and the shadows of dormant beliefs.

Start with presence: observe your physical sensations, your thoughts, and your emotions, without judgment. This practice, over time, reveals previously unseen patterns. For me, some years ago, it was recognizing a tenseness in my shoulders, a closing off of imagination when change approached—a leftover from earlier days when creativity was less regarded. Meeting this realization with understanding allowed me to reintegrate my creative spirit.

As you draw an understanding of the complete view of your reactions, you gain control and choose to pause and/or choose differently. In the past, when I would feel the old tension rise, I breathed deeply, inviting calm and opening the space for balanced reflection. Optimism resurfaces, and with it, visions of creative solutions previously hidden by doubt.

This journey into the self is ongoing, for life is an eternal teacher, revealing new dimensions at every turn. Embrace your emotions—they are proof of your profound capacity to feel. It's not about silencing them but about holding them in a compassionate light. From this foundation, pivot towards your deepest values with intention.

Building Social Connections as Collective Support

In the whirlwind of change, our bonds with others are our anchors. UCLA's research highlights the unparalleled stress-buffering power of social connections.

So, in this digital age, we should focus on strengthening our human networks. Value real interactions over virtual distractions. Share your visions and vulnerabilities about the future openly. Listen, support, and guide each other with empathy.

If loneliness has crept into your life, go beyond your comfort zone. Seek out communities that prioritize growth and societal advancement. My journey through personal unexpected showed me that shared challenges can forge deep, caring connections. Whether through local groups or online networks, find your tribe—your constellation of fellow supernovas—to navigate this journey together.

Globally, we must elevate our collective narrative—one that moves past divisions and unites us in our common humanity as we navigate the major shifts technology brings. Acknowledging our shared uncertainties creates solidarity, empowering us to offer understanding and support across communities.

An Invitation to Meet the Future

Instead of bracing against the tides of technological change, embrace your role as the jockey. How can you transform limiting beliefs into seeds of opportunity? How can you use self-awareness to consciously steer through the currents of change? How can you contribute to the mutual strength that empowers us all?

The future is a canvas yet unpainted, awaiting the bold strokes of those who dare to dream. Have faith, from darkness always comes the dawn. Have faith, in both your instincts and the bond with your friends. This is necessary to create a community where new ideas honor the worth of every individual. It's time for us to move ahead and to guide others on their journey.

18 Skills for Staying Ahead

In the exciting race that is "The Jockey on the Horse," the skilled jockey knows that staying ahead requires not only speed but also the foresight to anticipate the horse's next move. Similarly, in the ever-evolving landscape of artificial intelligence creatives must develop a repertoire of skills that allow them to partner with AI tools, ensuring that they ride alongside the wave of technological advancement rather than being left behind.

Futureproofing Creative Careers
In the fast-paced world of technology, where AI is making huge strides, the focus should not be on predicting the decline of human creativity, but on getting ready to work alongside AI in a collaborative manner. Similar to how past industrial revolutions improved living standards during changes we have the opportunity to guide how technology is integrated to ensure sustainable benefits, for all.

As the landscape evolves it's crucial for us to increase our understanding of not only technology and but also ethics. The ability to analyze data deeply as well as question biases embedded in algorithms created by organizations and governments, to then adjust to human-first norms, will define the new literacy of our era.

Specific Skills for the Creative Industry
To remain in the saddle, here are some skills available to get a strong understanding of:

- **Algorithm auditing**: Evaluate AI systems for biases and inaccuracies, ensuring they run the right course.
- **Data visualization literacy**: Transform complex data streams into insightful visual narratives.
- **Collaborative ideation**: Co-create with AI tools, sharing the reins of creativity rather than relying solely on them.
- **Hybrid media fluency**: Seamlessly blend physical realities with extended digital realms.
- **Tech policy reform advocacy**: Craft protections to ensure equitable access in the automated future.

- **AI ethics awareness**: Deepen your understanding of the opportunities and obligations AI presents.

Additional Key Skills for Creatives

As we prepare for the future, here are some additional skills to cultivate:

Soft Skills

- Cultural intelligence: Appreciate nuances across global markets that AI might miss.
- Design thinking: Center your innovation process around empathizing with human needs.
- Project management: Coordinate creative endeavors that span both physical and virtual realms.
- Entrepreneurial mindset: Spot commercial opportunities ahead of the AI curve.

Language and Writing

- Multilingual communication: Engage with markets beyond English-language content.
- Conversational UI writing: Script natural-sounding dialogue for digital assistants.
- Chip writing: Create compact audio brand identities for social media virality.
- Data storytelling: Weave compelling narratives from raw information.

Emerging Technical Fields

- Metaverse architecture: Design persistent virtual worlds that overlay our reality.
- Neural UX design: Craft intuitive and ethical user experiences for AI systems.
- Augmented content creation: Merge digital media with physical environments.
- Social token economy design: Build equitable blockchain incentive structures.

Adjacent Creative Roles

- AI photographer: Style generative models with a personal aesthetic.
- CGI fashion modeler: Visualize 3D garments with lifelike accuracy.
- Conversational writer: Script engaging dialogues for brand-specific chatbots.
- AR experience developer: Create immersive AR applications for mobile devices.

The Human Spark: Creativity's Enduring Future

The journey towards innovation requires not just expertise but also the insights gained from a reflective life. This is what truly ignites creativity. Our future leaders need to excel in the knowledge of the technology as well as have the ability to nurture emotional and spiritual qualities that algorithms cannot replicate.

What we are talking about is bravery that unites communities, compassion that touches the heart and foresight that envisions, beyond boundaries. These are the timeless sources of creativity that AI cannot ignite on its own. It's the leap, the significance that gives our work depth and connects to the essence of humanity.

In the symphony of creation, AI may be a powerful instrument, but it is the human spirit that creates the path, leading with a staff of ethical integrity and a vision written in the ink of compassion and imagination. As we embrace the tools of our time, let's do so with the wisdom of the jockey who knows the race is not just about the speed but the grace with which we navigate the course.

19 The Future of Work – Humans and AI Hand in Hand

In the journey of "The Jockey on the Horse," the harmonious partnership between the rider and their mount reflects a balance between control and synergy. It is a powerful metaphor for the future of work, where humans and machines labor in tandem, each enhancing the capabilities of the other, creating a harmony of productivity.

Microsoft's Satya Nadella paints an outlook where radical technologies don't replace but rather reshape industries, bringing to the workplace an era of sizeable reinvention. This chapter envisions a future where artificial intelligence doesn't overshadow human talent but instead amplifies it, where humans collaborate with AI, unlocking creative potential through the melding of our complementary abilities.

Augmenting Our Productivity

We are entering an era of "augmented intelligence," where technology is not a replacement but a magnifier of human creativity, emotional nuance, and ethical perspective. This paradigm shift sees technologies as partners, enhancing our innate talents and enabling us to reach tenfold our current potential.

From cyborg scientist Kevin Warwick, who melded his own body with technology, to startups like Otter.ai, which liberate workers from the drudgery of note-taking by summarizing meetings, we see glimpses of this new era. These examples demonstrate that augmentation is not just a theory but a practical reality enhancing our day-to-day lives.

The Case for Emotional Intelligence

While AI's capabilities grow, questions linger around its ability to understand the emotional and subtle nuances of human interaction. It is here that the symbiotic relationship between humans and computers finds its strength. AI can serve as a detailed advisor, but it is the human touch that guides it, applying wisdom and discernment to interpret and act on the data.

This collaboration ensures that while AI handles the repetitive tasks, humans can focus on what we excel at—emotional connections, creative synthesis, and innovative thinking. The future of work is not about offloading everything onto machines but about freeing up human potential to engage in meaningful and fulfilling activities.

Thriving Alongside AIs

As we ride the waves of change, we must adopt readiness strategies that enable us to not just survive but thrive amidst the disruptions of an AI-infused world. History shows us that with every industrial revolution comes new opportunities, and today's digital revolution calls forth a new class of digital designers, ethical engineers, and systems thinkers.

As we delve deeper into the symbiotic narrative of "The Jockey on the Horse," we consider the melding of human insight with artificial intelligence—a partnership that mirrors the understanding between a rider and their steed. The future of work doesn't just entail machines taking over but rather, them, amplifying our human capacities. This evolution is not just theoretical; it's already unfolding around us.

Real-Life Examples of AI and Human Collaboration

Ex. Augmenting Our Productivity

Take, for example, the legal profession. ROSS Intelligence, an AI-powered legal research tool, aids lawyers by sifting through thousands of case files to provide precise legal precedents, enhancing legal professionals' ability to draw insights. Yet, it's the lawyer's expertise that frames the questions and interprets the context—ROSS simply augments the grunt work.

Similarly, in healthcare, IBM's Watson helps doctors diagnose diseases by analyzing medical data at speeds and volumes impossible for a human. However, Watson isn't making the final diagnosis; doctors use its insights as a powerful adjunct to their medical acumen.

Ex. The Case for Emotional Intelligence

Looking back, we find historical examples of this blend of human-machine collaboration. During WWII, Alan Turing's Bombe machine automated the process of decoding Enigma, yet it was the cryptanalysts at Bletchley Park who provided the creative breakthroughs that led to deciphering the Axis powers' communications.

Today, customer service chatbots handle routine inquiries, allowing human agents to focus on complex issues requiring empathy and deeper understanding. This not only streamlines efficiency but elevates the quality of human interaction where it's most needed.

Ex. Thriving Alongside AIs

On the creative front, platforms like Canva use AI to suggest design templates and layouts, but it's the human eye that curates and customizes these suggestions to create a compelling visual story.

In the world of journalism, The New York Times uses an AI system called Editor to assist in identifying and correcting errors in articles before they reach human editors, enhancing the accuracy and reliability of news reporting.

Ex. Future-Proofing Work with AI

Looking to the future, companies like OpenAI have introduced tools like DALL·E, which creates images from textual descriptions, enhancing the creative process for artists and designers who can then build upon these AI-generated concepts with their unique style and vision.

This Shared Journey Continues

As we look at the course ahead, we must draw from these examples, seeing AI as a tool that unlocks human potential, not one that replaces it. The future of work, therefore, involves a continuous dance between leveraging AI's capabilities and enhancing our own, ensuring that as we harness this powerful technology, we remain the composers of our destiny.

As we embrace AI in our workplaces, we must ensure that the narrative remains one of partnership and progression, a journey not of replacement but of enhancement. The key to success in this new age will be our ability to integrate the strengths of AI with the irreplaceable qualities of human ingenuity, creativity, and emotional intelligence.

20 Educating for Tomorrow – My Vision

"The illiterate of the 21st century will not be those who cannot read and write, but those who cannot learn, unlearn, and relearn."
- ALVIN TOFFLER

In the realm of education teachers play a role, as both mentors and guides steering students, the leaders of tomorrow. Through the intricate pathways of an ever-evolving world. With a passion for education and a broad perspective that delves into the depths of learning psychology, to the forefront of trends, My life story includes many instances where I had to navigate through the complexities brought about by change. My journey is centered on unlocking potential through learning, flexibility and ethical creativity. Qualities vital, for those gearing up to navigate the seas of innovation impacting every industry.

This chapter crystallizes my vision for an educational transformation vital for gearing up the next generations for a future where their human skills will move in balance with the algorithms of AI, enhancing productivity in ways we can only begin to conceptualize.

Seismic Societal Shifts Underway

My journey across continents, engaging with myriad minds from students in classrooms to executives in boardrooms, has cemented my observation: a radical reinvention is underway. AI, like a generative force, is remolding human expression, and with it, the fabric of our society. Yet, for every voice that echoes the threat of automation and job extinction, visionary leaders are preparing the ground for a hybrid collaboration between humans and computers, expanding our collective capabilities.

The discerning question remains: Can synthetic systems emulate the emotional nuances that define the human experience? "Keep your hands on the reins," advises strategist Camilla Young, hinting at the inherent limits of AI (Lorraine, 2022. It is by merging the intuitive wisdom of humanity with the analytical prowess of AI that we will best navigate the future—a symbiotic race toward innovation.

Fostering Adaptability and Creativity

How do we prepare our students to surf the tidal waves of change rather than be swept away? Historical revolutions birthed new classes of artisans who creatively steered the winds of change. Today calls for the digital artisans, ethical engineers, and systemic thinkers to direct the course of innovation towards empowerment rather than domination.

Beyond the confines of traditional technical training lies the expansive field of cultural intelligence, critical thinking, and moral imagination. It is these skills, interwoven like the strands of a finely braided rope, that will enable the youth to harness AI's potential responsibly. For the values and decisions encoded in algorithms, today will ripple through the social fabric for generations to come.

Fostering Thriving Interconnected

As industries evolve, there will be displacement, but this is the nature of creative destruction. It paves the way for a renaissance of human ingenuity, where roles dependent solely on productivity give way to careers centered around human connection, creativity, and wisdom—domains where technology alone cannot tread.

Let's imagine an education that brings together the strands of diverse disciplines, creating a canvas strong enough to cover the large expanse of an AI-integrated future. It is our collective output that will write inventions that give importance to equity while not compromising innovation, balancing the new digital code with the timeless virtues of humanity.

Fostering Adaptable Learners

In the era of AI, 'learning how to learn' becomes the key to flexibility. Like a jockey adept at riding different horses, students must become fluent in the language of change, equipped with the adaptability to embrace new careers that will inevitably emerge from the unknown future.

Let's draw from the beginnings of Renaissance thinkers, who, with their wide-ranging curiosities, cross-trained their intellect across various disciplines. In a similar vein, adaptability springs from a rich mosaic of experiences spanning the arts and sciences, storytelling, and computational thinking.

The Choice Lies Before Us

As we stand before the coming horizon, we must decide how to build the narrative of progress. Will our collective wisdom guide AI to serve the greater good, to amplify prosperity inclusively? The path we choose now will set the course for the digital horses of tomorrow. Let's, with intention for good, guide this powerful force to augment and elevate, not to diminish or divide.

In this chapter, we will explore these themes further, examining how we, as educators, can cultivate a fertile ground for growth, preparing our students to take the lead and ride confidently into the Age of AI.

21 Beyond Fear - Positive Narratives Around AI

"Though we cannot direct the wind, we can adjust the sails."
- ANONYMOUS

The age-old saying highlights our capacity to adapt to the changes, around us—a metaphor that resonates deeply with our exploration of intelligence. AI like the wind serves as an element in today's digital landscape driving us towards a future beyond the imagination of our predecessors. This segment delves into embracing this phenomenon not with fear but like a rider guiding a mighty steed, towards triumph.

Harnessing Innate Creativity Amidst Technological Tides

As we encounter the winds of advancement we see society standing at a moment of past societies that were apprehensive, about the introduction of automobiles. However, where there is a disruption, in the way of life there also lies an opening—a possibility to unlock our capabilities from the monotony of life and potential hazards. This section honors individuals who are not merely resisting the wave of AI. Rather navigating it with the skill and grace of a rider., upskilling their uniquely human strengths to stride confidently into new possibilities.

Embracing Symbiosis: The Jockey and the AI Steed

In the realm of automation anxiety, thought leaders anticipate less turmoil and more collaboration. Don Norman, a visionary in design, imagines an era where human expertise and AI capabilities entwine, creating a symbiotic relationship that enhances both parties. Like a jockey and horse in perfect harmony, startups like Fireflies.ai demonstrate how AI can take on the routine, leaving us free to engage in the higher-order thinking that defines our humanity. Here, we are reminded that while AI navigates the terrain, it is the jockey who provides direction, guiding with wisdom and experience that machines have yet to master.

Charting New Courses: Creativity as Our Compass

As we pivot from "what is" to "what could be," we see how our creative faculties are not overshadowed by AI but are instead given new platforms to shine. The creative soul of humanity cannot be replicated by algorithms; it is this soul that dreams up the previously inconceivable, turning science fiction into science fact. This chapter will explore how, with AI representing the force of change, we can chart new courses, emboldened by the possibility of augmented intelligence, yet grounded by the knowledge that consciousness is our realm alone.

Reimagining Our Place in the Digital Gallop

Proactive reskilling and reimagination are the reins by which we maintain control in the digital journey. History has shown us that disruption heralds not the end but the beginning of new artistry. In this era, it calls for digitally literate thinkers who can steer the course of AI toward a future that benefits all, not just the few. This chapter will delve into how, beyond technical skill, our cultural intelligence, foresight, and ethics will set us apart as we consciously cultivate a future ripe with abundance.

Educational Evolution: Riding Towards Inclusivity

The youngest among us—digital natives—are acutely aware of the legacies of power that threaten to deplete our collective resources. Yet, they are the torchbearers of change, holding institutions accountable and championing inclusive education. Programs like Kenzie Academy are exemplars, expanding access to technological literacy, and ensuring that students are not competing with machines but synergizing with them, blending the strengths of man with the precision of AI. As these students emerge as adept communicators and culturally responsive thinkers, they embody the very essence of adaptability, essential for navigating the evolving landscape of employment.

Uniting for Empowerment: The Collective Sprint

Beyond individual initiatives, a greater movement is happening, one that binds creative minds, humanitarians, and tech pioneers in a shared sprint toward empowerment. This chapter will highlight how networks such as those spearheaded by the Henry Luce Foundation foster grassroots innovation, proving that when we invest in local ingenuity, we plant the seeds of stability and growth. From upcycling projects to VR-assisted education, we witness the rise of initiatives that serve the underserved, driven by a vision of what can be achieved when we move as one.

The Future Calls with Open Arms

Let's welcome this era of AI advancement with the bravery ingrained in our nature. As we become aware of the pressing needs, within our communities, it is our duty to share innovations and knowledge guaranteeing that everyone progresses together. The pathway to tomorrow is clear and, through unity, ethical vision and steadfast resolve we can all move forward harmoniously. "The best way to predict your future is to create it," said Abraham Lincoln. Let this be our manifesto as we, the jockeys of our destiny, take the reins and guide our steed, AI, toward a future defined by dignity, opportunity, and uninhibited creativity.

22 Embracing the Uncertain Future

"In a time where the future stretches out like a horizon, a jockey must look ahead drawing lessons from the trail traveled while remaining open, to the obstacles that lie ahead." This belief, echoing the wisdom of George Santayana, resonates particularly in today's fast-paced AI growth and its impact on society. As we explore this landscape our shared strength relies on our capacity to adjust to ongoing shifts not with apprehension but, with a proactive approach and a steadfast ethical guide.

Learning Flexibility from Renaissance Trailblazers

The Renaissance, a time of explosive intellectual expansion, offers us enduring lessons on adaptability. Leonardo Da Vinci, a polymath who seamlessly transitioned between diverse disciplines, stands as a beacon of versatility and innovation. His life teaches us that the essence of adaptability lies not in rigidly adhering to one path but in the fluidity of transitioning across multiple passions with an open heart and an agile mind.

Da Vinci's life was one of constant learning and relearning, his adaptability enabling him to thrive through various seasons of his career. His example brightens the path for today's trailblazers, urging us to embrace the Renaissance spirit of lifelong learning and cross-disciplinary exploration, especially as we navigate the unpredictable waves of technological advancement.

Cultivating Versatility in the Exponential Era

In the variety of today's innovators, figures like AI pioneer Vivienne Ming stand out, showcasing the importance of transcending specialized silos. Ming's career, though rooted in theoretical neuroscience, has spanned across multiple domains, reflecting the same versatility and hunger for knowledge that drove Da Vinci. This adaptability is crucial for today's learners and leaders, as it prepares them to pivot and thrive in a future where roles and industries are rapidly evolving.

Building Change Muscles as Innovation Accelerates

As we brace for the accelerating pace of AI-driven change, it becomes imperative to develop societal "change muscles"—the collective flexibility to adapt to the disruptions poised to reshape entire sectors. This requires foresight and collaborative governance to steer the course of technology in ways that preserve our humanistic values. Much like the jockey who guides the horse with expertise and gentle command, we must lead the age of AI with a balance of wisdom and ethical insight.

Letting Ethics Be the Lighthouse in the Storm

In the face of this whirlwind of change, it is our unwavering ethical foundations that will serve as our North Star, helping us to stay the course. It is these principles that will anchor us amidst the storms of uncertainty and propel us forward with the strong momentum of innovation.

23 Cultivating the Abundant Mindset

Life has a way of conditioning us to develop a mentality of scarcity - there is never enough time, money, opportunities, or resources to go around. We become focused on what we lack rather than the gifts we have been given. Shifting to an abundant mindset opens up new possibilities and allows us to fully tap into our innate gifts and talents.

The Scarcity Trap
The scarcity mindset stems from a place of fear rather than faith. We view everything in our life from the lens of "There is not enough" rather than "There is more than enough." This focuses our mind on restriction rather than the expansive nature of possibility. We define ourselves by our limits rather than our gifts which cuts off our creativity.

Turning Scarce into Plentiful
The shift from scarcity to abundance begins with gratitude. When we express genuine appreciation for what we have been given - our health, family, and friends, opportunities that come our way - we begin to train our minds to expect more gifts in the future. Gratitude opens up space for greater joy, inspiration, meaningful work, and all manifestations of abundance.

Faith is also key - whether belief in a higher power or belief in the human capacity for creative expansion. Having faith that we are part of an abundant, giving universe liberates us from fear and allows us to boldly develop our talents to benefit others. We instinctively know our creative gifts are meant for the betterment of the whole.

Recognizing Gifts and Talents
Abundance does not mean we stretch ourselves thin trying to develop every talent imaginable. It means recognizing our special, innate gifts and nurturing them. Intuition is a powerful compass here. What creative activities leave you feeling energized and fulfilled? What skills seem to come easily and naturally? These are clues toward your inherent talents meant to be cultivated.

Make a list of areas in which you display natural talent such as art, writing, connecting people, designing systems, leading teams, etc. Recognize abundance you may take for granted like athletic ability, mathematical or scientific skills, musical ability, business acumen, and so on. Determine a few standout strengths to focus on rather than spreading yourself too thin.

Cultivating Purpose and Possibility

Living a purpose-driven life generates abundance and opportunity. When our special talents are used productively to serve real needs, we are rewarded with meaningful work. Tending to the betterment of our communities, society and world makes living feel more worthwhile.

There is an energy of joyful creativity, enthusiasm, and zeal when we utilize our talents toward a purpose bigger than ourselves. Ideas flow freely, collaborators and resources line up, and encouragement and support show up just when needed. By cultivating a vision focused on collective good, we tap into the realm of unlimited possibility thinking rather than limits and lack.

The abundant mindset recognizes that scarcity exists amidst immense bounty, darkness amidst immeasurable light. Our minds overflow with gifts meant to uplift the world. As we orient to this truth and boldly develop our creativity, we fulfill our highest calling.

24 Boosting Creativity and Possibility Thinking

Cultivating the Seeds of Creativity

In the heart of every individual lies a wellspring of creativity, often untapped or stifled by the constructs of conventional thinking. Just as an acorn holds the potential of a towering oak, every person carries within them gifts that can burgeon into extraordinary ideas and achievements. "We must never forget that we may also find meaning in life, even when confronted with a hopeless situation when facing a fate that cannot be changed," wrote Viktor E. Frankl in 'Man's Search for Meaning'. It is within this space of seemingly insurmountable challenges that creativity becomes not just an asset but a necessity.

Unleashing Our Innate Gifts

Our first step in harnessing creativity is recognizing that it is not a finite resource but a renewable energy that can be cultivated and expanded. Elizabeth Gilbert, in 'Big Magic: Creative Living Beyond Fear', invites us to embrace our curiosity and let go of needless fear. "You can measure your worth by your dedication to your path, not by your successes or failures," she writes, encouraging a journey of continuous creative exploration.

Case Study: The Renaissance of Creativity in AI

Consider the renaissance of creativity in the age of AI, where machines can learn to paint, compose music, and write poetry. While some view this as a threat to human artistry, it can also be seen as a catalyst for human creativity. AI algorithms have created artworks that have sold for hundreds of thousands of dollars, not to replace human art, but to push the boundaries of what art can be. These collaborations between man and machine, rather than diminishing our creative spirit, can amplify it.

Envisioning Positive Futures

Envisioning positive futures is akin to planting a garden of possibilities. It's a conscious exercise in optimism, where we design our aspirations with intention. The Stanford D. School, known for its innovative approach to design thinking, champions the power of a positive mindset to envision new solutions and products. They advocate for a step called "How might we...", which shifts the dialogue from problem-focused to solution-oriented, empowering creators to think without limits.

Moving from "What Is" to "What Could Be"

The journey from "what is" to "what could be" requires a pivot in perspective. Instead of seeing AI as a force that renders human effort redundant, we can choose to view it as a tool that complements and enhances human capability. For example, IBM's Watson can analyze vast quantities of medical data to assist doctors in diagnosing diseases. This isn't replacing the doctors; it's augmenting their ability to heal.

Creating a Culture of Possibility Thinkers

To foster a culture of possibility thinkers, we must encourage an educational system that values creative risk-taking and celebrates innovative failures as much as successes. The Google X laboratory, known for its 'moonshot' projects, operates under the belief that failure is a necessary step towards groundbreaking innovation. Astro Teller, the head of X, encourages teams to "fail fast" and learn from each setback, a principle that fuels their creative process.

The Infinite Canvas of the Future

As we embrace AI and integrate it into the fabric of our lives, let's see it as an extension of our creativity. Let's use it to paint on the infinite canvas of the future, where our collective imagination shapes a world that reflects our highest aspirations. I ask you to join me in this dance of possibility thinking, where together with AI, we choreograph a future that resonates with the beauty of our innermost creative spirits. "The future belongs to those who believe in the beauty of their dreams," Eleanor Roosevelt once said. Let our dreams, amplified by AI, guide us into a future vibrant with potential and rich with fulfillment.

Part IV:
Exercises and Activities

25 Reflections and Exercises: Building Resilience and a Positive Mindset

Ideas and Activities for Embracing Change

1. Reflect on Adaptability: Recall a time when a significant change led to personal growth. What did you learn about yourself? How did you adapt?
2. Cultivate a Growth Mindset: Practice reframing thoughts that embody a fixed mindset ("I can't do this") to those that encourage growth ("I can learn to do this with time and effort").
3. Stress-Management Plan: Develop a personal stress-management plan. Include activities such as exercise, meditation, or journaling that help you maintain a sense of calm amidst change.
4. Declutter Your Life: Choose an area of your life to declutter. This could be your physical environment, your commitments, or even your digital space. Notice how this act impacts your mental clarity.
5. Craft Your Dance with Change: Write a personal vision statement that embraces change. How will you move with it, grow with it, and flourish within it?

In every moment of uncertainty, remember that you are the author of your own story. Allow these exercises be your guide as you develop a narrative of resilience, adaptability, and hope. Let this dance with change be a beautiful one.

26 Reflection Activities for Optimizing a Positive Mindset

As we continue to navigate the exciting and sometimes daunting realm of AI, it's crucial to engage in activities that enhance our understanding and shape our perspective positively. Like a jockey who reflects after every race to improve their synergy with their horse, we too must take the time to reflect on and refine our relationship with AI. These exercises, activities, and thought-provoking questions are designed to foster an optimistic outlook on AI and its role in our lives.

Activity 1: Discovering Your Creative AI Partner
Objective: To identify areas in your life where AI can serve as a creative partner.
Exercise: Make a list of daily tasks that consume time but require little creative thought. Next, research and write down AI tools that could assist with these tasks.
Reflection: How does freeing up this time with AI help you increase your creative output? What new creative pursuits could you explore with this extra time?

Activity 2: Envisioning Your AI-Assisted Future
Objective: To imagine a future where AI enhances your personal and professional life.
Exercise: Write a short narrative or create a vision board that illustrates a day in your life five years from now, with AI seamlessly integrated into your routine.
Reflection: How does this envisioned future feel? What steps can you take now to make this vision a reality?

Activity 3: Shifting Perspectives
Objective: To practice shifting from a mindset of "what is" to "what could be" with AI.
Exercise: Think of a current challenge in your workplace or community. Brainstorm how AI could transform this challenge into an opportunity.

Reflection: How does changing your perspective affect your approach to problem-solving? Can you identify any limiting beliefs that might be holding back your creativity?

Activity 4: The AI Ethics Dialogue

Objective: To engage in ethical considerations surrounding AI.

Exercise: Host a discussion group or debate to explore the ethical implications of AI in society. Use case studies or news articles as a starting point for conversation.

Reflection: What new insights did you gain from this dialogue?

How can you apply these insights to promote ethical AI use?

Activity 5: Lifelong Learning Plan

Objective: To create a plan for continuous learning and adaptation in the age of AI.

Exercise: Develop a personal learning roadmap that includes acquiring new skills, attending workshops, or taking courses related to AI and emerging technologies.

Reflection: How does committing to lifelong learning affect your confidence in navigating the future with AI?

Activity 6: The AI Inclusivity Workshop

Objective: To conceptualize how AI can be used to foster inclusivity and equality.

Exercise: Design a workshop aimed at creating AI solutions that address inclusivity issues. Consider aspects such as accessibility, bias in AI, and cultural sensitivity.

Reflection: How can AI be leveraged to create more inclusive environments in your community or industry?

Your AI Narrative

JOCKEY ON THE HORSE

Each race, each round of training with AI as your horse, builds your story as a jockey. Similarly, every exercise and reflection in this chapter contributes to your personal narrative around AI. As you complete these activities, you're not just passively consuming information about AI—you're actively shaping a future where technology elevates human potential and creativity. Remember, the reins are in your hands, and with thoughtful guidance, you and AI can cross the finish line together, champions of innovation and progress.

27 Exercises and Reflections to Direct the Future

The Stepping Stones of Change

As we embrace the uncertain future, it is vital to engage in exercises that not only reinforce our understanding of change but also equip us with practical tools to navigate it. This chapter is designed to complement the insights shared previously, offering actionable steps, reflective questions, and exercises to embed the principles of resilience, adaptability, and optimism into the very fabric of our being.

Activity 1: Belief Mapping

Objective: Identify and transform limiting beliefs about uncertainty into empowering ones.

1. List your top five fears about the future.
2. Challenge each fear with evidence: Is this fear based on facts or assumptions?
3. Reframe each fear into a positive statement or question that opens possibilities.
4. Commit to one action that aligns with your new, empowering belief.

Reflection Questions:

- What new opportunities can arise from this change that wouldn't have been possible before?
- How can this belief serve as a stepping stone rather than a stumbling block?

Activity 2: The Flexibility Routine

Objective: Build cognitive flexibility by introducing variability into your daily life.

1. Choose one routine task each day.

2. Alter it in a small way (e.g., if you usually read tech news first, start with world news instead).
3. Reflect on how this small change affected your day and your adaptability.

Reflection Questions:

- Did the change in routine make you feel uncomfortable or refreshed? Why?
- What did this teach you about your capacity to adapt to larger changes?

Activity 3: Mindful Awareness Practice

Objective: Cultivate self-knowledge to respond consciously to change.

1. Set aside 10 minutes for a mindfulness meditation focusing on your breath.
2. Whenever you notice your mind wandering to the future, gently bring it back to the present.
3. Afterward, write down any thoughts about the future that persistently arose.

Reflection Questions:

- What patterns do you notice in your thoughts about the future?
- How can you apply this awareness to respond more consciously in daily life?

Activity 4: Connection Web

Objective: Strengthen social connections to build a support network for navigating change.

1. Draw a web and place yourself at the center.
2. Add spokes leading out to the people who support you.
3. Reach out to at least one person in your web this week to discuss your thoughts about the future.

Reflection Questions:

- How did the conversation impact your feelings about the future?
- What steps can you take to strengthen these connections further?

Activity 5: The Optimism Journal
Objective: Foster a habit of optimism in viewing the future.

1. Every evening, write down three things about the future you are optimistic about.
2. Reflect on why these aspects excite you and how they align with your values.
3. Once a week, review your entries and notice any patterns or themes.

Reflection Questions:

- How does this exercise impact your overall outlook on the future?
- Which aspects of the future consistently bring you hope, and why?

Activity 6: The Scenario Sandbox
Objective: Engage with the uncertainty of the future through creative thinking.

1. Imagine three different future scenarios based on current technological trends.
2. For each scenario, write down how society could adapt positively.
3. Consider what role you could play in each of these potential futures.

Reflection Questions:

- Which of your skills and passions are applicable in these scenarios?
- How does envisioning these possibilities make you feel about the future?

As you engage with these activities, embrace them, learn from them, and let them guide you toward a future abundant with hope and success. Carry forward as a supernova, lighting up the path not only for yourself but for all who journey alongside you.

28 Supplemental Exercises for Future Mapping in and Out of the Office

Exercise: Charting Your Path

1. Objective: To map out personal and professional goals in an AI-integrated future.
2. Task: Reflect on your current career path or life direction. Imagine how it might evolve with AI advancements. Outline the steps you could take to align with these changes.
3. Outcome: Create a "Future Map" that includes potential roles, skills needed, and ethical considerations for your journey ahead.

Activity: Scenario Planning Workshop

1. Objective: To anticipate and prepare for various AI-driven future scenarios.
2. Task: Assemble a team and develop several scenarios of how AI could change your industry. For each scenario, discuss potential responses and strategies.
3. Outcome: Produce a guidebook for your industry's AI future, providing insights and action plans for various potential outcomes.

Reflection: Ethics in AI

1. Objective: To deepen understanding of the ethical implications of AI.
2. Task: Consider ethical dilemmas that AI might present in your field. Write a reflective essay or create a presentation discussing these issues.
3. Outcome: Share your findings with peers or through a blog post, sparking further discussion on the importance of ethics in the age of AI.

Activity: Lifelong Learning Plan

1. Objective: To commit to continuous learning in the face of technological change.

2. Task: Identify areas in which you need to grow to keep pace with AI. Research courses, workshops, or resources that can help you in these areas.

3. Outcome: Create a "Lifelong Learning Ledger" that tracks your progress and reflects on the learning experiences over time.

Riding Into Tomorrow

Let these exercises and reflections guide you as you step confidently into the future. With the reins of AI firmly in hand, Let's ride into tomorrow not with anxiety but with the excitement of explorers on the cusp of a new world. We can choose our journey to be guided by the persistent light of ethical principles and the spirit of continuous growth and adaptability. Together, as jockeys of innovation, we will chart a course through the uncertain future, turning the unknown into a landscape of infinite opportunity.

29 Your Interactive Guide to Harness Generative AI

As we continue our journey in "The Jockey on the Horse," where you've learned to grasp the reins in the ever-evolving landscape of AI. With fashion as a use case, let's put your knowledge into practice. Just as a jockey must become one with their horse, understanding its nuances and strengths, so too must you become familiar with the tools and capabilities of Generative AI. This supplemental guide provides quizzes, activities, and exercises to help you engage actively with Generative AI and make it an integral part of your creative arsenal.

As the jockey intuitively feels the horse's movements beneath them, guiding it with expertise and foresight, let's transition from theory to application, ensuring that your ride into the future of AI-amplified fashion or creativity is not just assured, but a winning one.

Quiz: Test Your Generative AI Knowledge

1. What is Generative AI, and how is it used in fashion design?
2. Name at least two Generative AI tools that fashion designers can use.
3. Explain how Generative AI might impact sustainability in fashion.
4. Describe one way Generative AI can personalize fashion for consumers.

Activity: Generative AI Design Challenge

1. Objective: Use a Generative AI tool to create a new pattern or design.
2. Task: Select a Generative AI platform and input your design parameters. Experiment with different inputs to see how the AI interprets your creative prompts.
3. Outcome: Share your AI-generated designs on social media or with your peers, explaining your process and the AI's role in your final product.

A Fun Exercise: Crafting an AI-Assisted Fashion Campaign

1. Objective: Conceptualize a fashion campaign incorporating Generative AI.
2. Steps:
a. Outline the theme of your campaign.
b. Detail how you would use Generative AI for the visuals, such as the models, outfits, or setting.
c. Describe the story you want to tell through this AI-assisted campaign.
3. Reflection: How does incorporating Generative AI change the creative process and the storytelling potential of your campaign?

Activity: Generative AI and Sustainability Workshop

1. Objective: Explore Generative AI's potential to drive sustainability in fashion.
2. Task: Host a brainstorming session to identify ways Generative AI could reduce waste or improve efficiency in production.
3. Outcome: Develop a small presentation or report outlining your sustainable solutions powered by Generative AI.

Exercise: Your First Steps with Generative AI

1. Objective: Get hands-on experience with Generative AI.
2. Action Items
a. Sign up for a Generative AI platform.
b. Complete a tutorial on creating a simple design or pattern.
c. Reflect on the experience and jot down three ways Generative AI could impact your design process.

Upskilling with Generative AI

1. Objective: Develop a plan for integrating Generative AI into your skillset.
2. Steps:
a. Research online courses that teach Generative AI basics.

b. Set a goal for what you want to achieve with Generative AI in the next six months.

c. Create a weekly learning schedule that allows time for both study and practical application.

With each stride, the jockey learns more about their horse, building a relationship of mutual respect and understanding. Similarly, as you complete these activities, you will develop a deeper relationship with Generative AI, learning to harness its capabilities to enhance your creativity and expand the boundaries of fashion design. Together, you will race toward a future where technology and human ingenuity create a new standard of beauty and innovation.

30 Practical Exercises for Future-Ready Learning

Introduction: Setting the Pace

As educators, we are not only imparters of knowledge but also the architects of learning experiences that prepare our students to harness the power of AI. Like jockeys attuning to their horses' strengths, we must align our teaching strategies with the evolving capabilities of our students. This set of exercises is designed to reinforce the concepts of adaptability, ethical engagement, and creative collaboration with AI.

Activity 1: Mapping the AI Landscape

Objective: To develop a foundational understanding of AI's role in various sectors.

Exercise: Research and create a map outlining current and potential uses of AI in different industries. Note how AI complements human roles in these scenarios.

Reflection: How does understanding the broader AI landscape affect your perception of its capabilities and limitations?

Activity 2: The Unlearning Challenge

Objective: To practice the art of unlearning outdated information and relearning with a fresh perspective.

Exercise: Choose a belief or practice within your field that has been altered by new technology. Actively seek out and engage with resources that challenge this old paradigm.

Reflection: What resistance did you encounter internally while unlearning? How did the relearning process shift your perspective?

Activity 3: Emotional Intelligence in the Age of AI

Objective: To recognize the irreplaceable value of human emotional intelligence in an AI-driven world.

Exercise: Participate in or facilitate a role-playing activity that requires empathy, such as conflict resolution or collaborative storytelling, and identify the nuances that AI currently cannot replicate.

Reflection: In what ways does this exercise highlight the unique contributions of human sensitivity and creativity?

Activity 4: The Ethical Compass

Objective: To explore the ethical implications of AI and cultivate moral imagination.

Exercise: Develop a set of ethical guidelines for AI use in your area of expertise. Consider privacy, equity, and the long-term impacts of AI decisions.

Reflection: How does creating these guidelines inform your sense of responsibility as a "jockey" guiding the "horse" of AI?

Activity 5: Adaptability Workouts

Objective: To strengthen the 'adaptability muscles' needed to thrive alongside AI.

Exercise: Engage in a new activity or learn a new skill outside your comfort zone every month, reflecting on the learning process and how it can apply to staying adaptable in the face of AI advancements.

Reflection: How do these 'workouts' enhance your ability to embrace change?

Activity 6: Cross-Disciplinary Journeys

Objective: To foster cross-disciplinary thinking and understand the interconnectedness of knowledge in the age of AI.

Exercise: Collaborate with someone from a different field to solve a problem, merging your expertise with theirs to find innovative solutions.

Reflection: What insights did this cross-disciplinary approach uncover that a single-field perspective might have missed?

Here are some exercises and questions to complement to help you cultivate an abundant mindset:

31 Cultivating Abundance: Reflection and Practice

The previous chapter explored shifting from a scarcity mentality to an abundant mindset that taps into our gifts and creative potential. This chapter contains questions and exercises to help apply those concepts to your own life and develop greater abundance:

Check-In Questions
- What areas currently cause you to think from a lacking or limited mindset? Finances? Time? Creative ideas? Relationships?
- How might gratitude shift your perspective in those domains? Make a list of 3-5 things right now you are grateful for. How does your outlook change?
- What activities and interests leave you feeling alive and energized? What talents seem to arise naturally?

Get Curious About Your Talents
- Make a master list of all types of intelligence and abilities - music, math, physicality, creativity, strategy, empathy, etc. Check the ones you possess even if underdeveloped.
- Ask friends and family what special skills and strengths they notice in you. So often we are blind to our own gifts.
- Notice what creative activities you gravitate toward in your spare time for clues about innate talents waiting to emerge.

Cultivate Your Talents
- Choose 1-2 standout talents you currently underutilize. Commit to developing them with daily practice.
- Stay curious: What skills come easily to you? What meaningful activities lose track of time? These are signs of innate gifts to cultivate.
- Determine specific next steps to devote time to developing talents.

Join groups, take lessons, and start projects.

Live On Purpose

- Identify people and causes that spark compassion and concern within you. Your purpose likely connects to serving these domains.
- Brainstorm imaginative ideas to contribute to these areas of care using your strengths and resources.
- Take one small step to act on this sense of purpose. Fulfillment generates further inspiration and abundance!

By getting curious about our talents and taking purposeful action, we shift from lack to creative potential. An abundant mindset awakens courage, compassion, and creativity waiting to manifest through our unique gifts!

The Victory Lap

By engaging in these activities, you will not only solidify your understanding of AI's transformative potential but also cultivate the skills necessary to navigate the future with confidence. As educators, we set the pace for our students' journeys, equipping them with the resilience and foresight needed to embrace tomorrow's challenges. Remember, it is not the swiftest horse that wins the race, but the one most responsive to its rider's guidance.

Let's guide our learners with intention and wisdom, ensuring that as the world of AI evolves, they too will adapt, grow, and ultimately, triumph.

Part V:
AI and the New Creative Process from Fashion to Music and Beyond

32 The Creative Toolbox: AI Tools for Fashion, Visual Arts, Writing, and Beyond

In the context of personalization in fashion, AI tools can be used to create custom patterns for textiles, allowing brands to offer one-of-a-kind products that resonate with their customers' preferences and styles. Some of these AI tools include:

FASHION
1. VisualHound: VisualHound is an AI tool specifically tailored for fashion designers, providing a unique platform for prototyping designs before they enter production. It creates realistic-looking product images to feed mood boards and streamline the design process, allowing designers to experiment with various patterns and styles.
2. Silic AI: Silic AI is a generative fashion tool that creates personalized designs in seconds and offers suggested prompts. It is designed to assist designers in creating custom patterns and unique textile designs that align with their creative vision and brand identity.
3. Designovel: Designovel is an AI fashion designer tool that utilizes generative AI, employing techniques like metric learning and multi- modal embedding to create content that aligns with current fashion trends, styles, and brands. It provides valuable insights into current fashion trends, aiding users in making informed decisions quickly and efficiently. The tool offers a range of solutions, including trend analysis, forecasting, and market sensing for product and service planning, all powered by its advanced fashion AI world.
4. Kidgeni: Kidgeni is an AI art creator for kids to create art that they can wear. It offers a platform for creating custom patterns and unique textile designs, allowing children to express their creativity and individuality through personalized fashion creations.
5. DeepFashion: Fashion Assistant is an AI-powered tool that offers personalized outfit recommendations based on users' wardrobe items. It leverages AI to provide users with a seamless way to make informed fashion choices.

These AI tools are at the forefront of leveraging AI to create custom patterns for textiles, allowing brands to offer one-of-a-kind products that align with their customers' preferences and styles. They provide designers with valuable insights, streamline the design process, and offer a wide range of possibilities for creating unique and personalized textile designs.

IMAGE GENERATORS

Several AI tools and companies are utilizing AI to create visually stunning and emotionally resonant images. Some of the notable tools are known for their ability to produce high-quality and detailed images, making them suitable for creative professionals and enthusiasts.

For creative professionals and enthusiasts looking to generate stunning images using AI tools, three top options include Midjourney, Leonardo AI, and Adobe Firefly. Each of these tools offers unique features and capabilities tailored to different needs and artistic visions.

1. Midjourney: Midjourney is an advanced AI image generator that gained significant attention for its ability to create highly detailed and realistic images. It operates through a Discord interface, requiring users to have a Discord account and subscribe to access its features. Midjourney is particularly noted for producing photorealistic images with impressive attention to detail, including accurate reflections, shadows, and textures. This tool is ideal for users looking for advanced image-generation capabilities.

2. Leonardo AI: Leonardo AI stands out for its powerful performance and customization options. It offers a professional interface with multiple models catering to different artistic needs. Users can customize images with a high degree of granularity, setting resolutions up to 2688×2688 pixels, choosing the number of outputs, and adjusting the depth of the images.

3. Photosonic: Photosonic is highlighted as a platform suitable for digital marketers who want to create AI imagery to complement AI-optimized content.

4. Fotor's AI Image Generator: Known for its user-friendly interface and the ability to create striking images with vivid colors and realistic textures. It also provides various other tools such as an AI photo editor, background remover, graphic designer, and collage maker.

5. NightCafe: This tool offers an expansive palette of customization, catering to a spectrum of art styles, from abstract musings to lifelike portraits. It allows users to have extensive control over the image generation process, making it suitable for a creative audience.

6. DALL-E 3: DALL-E 3 is an advanced AI image generator built to craft detailed and lifelike images from text prompts. It seamlessly integrates text into the generated images, solving a long-standing AI challenge. This tool is ideal for creative professionals, brands aiming to visually represent their vision, and day-to-day users keen on AI-powered image generation.

7. Shutterstock: Shutterstock's AI tool is making waves in the design and marketing industry. It is like having a magic wand to whip up stunning visuals in a snap, supercharging campaigns with AI-crafted images, and providing a seemingly endless pool of unique shots. This tool is beneficial for designers, marketers, and content creators looking for distinct visuals for their material.

8. Adobe Firefly: Adobe Firefly, currently in beta, provides AI for graphic designers to create images, transform text, and play with color using simple text prompts. It offers AI for graphic designers to create images, transform text, and play with color using simple text prompts. It is accessible within the Adobe platform and can be used to take on some of the time-consuming, manual aspects of design.

9. Visme: Visme's text-to-image generation tool is free, easy to use, and powerful, generating visuals out of plain text input. It is ideal for anyone who wants to generate copyright-free realistic and detailed AI-generated images.

10. Craiyon: Craiyon is an AI model that creates images from text. Users enter a text prompt of what they want to see, and Craiyon creates it. It is a light version of OpenAI's DALL-E and is helpful for professionals working in marketing, graphic design, and fine art.

These tools and companies are at the forefront of leveraging AI to create visually stunning and emotionally resonant images that align perfectly with specific briefs' look and feel. They offer a wide range of possibilities for creative professionals, designers, and brands aiming to visually represent their vision.

INTERIOR DESIGN

Several AI tools are available for room layouts, furniture placement, and color schemes. These tools are designed to assist interior designers, architects, and individuals in optimizing space planning and creating personalized design solutions. Some of the notable AI tools in this domain include:

1. RoomGPT: RoomGPT is a user-friendly AI tool that generates semi-realistic renderings based on user inputs. It allows users to upload an image of an existing space, choose the room type, and specify the design style. The system then generates two AI iterations of the design, providing visual inspiration for design enthusiasts.
2. Runway ML: Runway ML is a machine learning toolkit that enables artists and designers to experiment with AI and create new visual content. The platform offers a wide range of tools and models that can be used to generate images, videos, and interactive experiences, providing new possibilities for creative expression.
3. PlanFinder: PlanFinder is an AI architecture floor plan generator that can analyze a space's dimensions and offer optimal design solutions within seconds. It suggests furniture arrangements, color schemes, and allows users to experiment with various design concepts.
4. Homestyler: Homestyler is an AI-powered interior design tool that offers a comprehensive set of features for room layout planning and realistic 3D rendering. It leverages advanced AI algorithms to assist designers in every step of the design process, including furniture placement and layout optimization.
5. Foyr Neo: Foyr Neo is an AI-driven tool that specializes in creating realistic 3D renderings and high-quality 3D models. It leverages cutting-edge AI algorithms to generate textures, lighting effects, and accurate furniture placement, offering enhanced visualization capabilities for designers.

These AI tools are designed to streamline the design process, save time, and offer personalized design solutions for interior designers, architects, and individuals. By leveraging these tools, designers can experiment with various design concepts, optimize space planning, and visualize their ideas more accurately, ultimately enhancing the overall design process.

AI's impact extends to music production, where it has been used to create new and innovative sounds. Artists and musicians have employed AI-generated music to explore novel compositions and push the boundaries of traditional music creation. These examples illustrate the diverse applications of AI in fostering creativity across various artistic disciplines.

MUSIC

AI music generators offer creatives the ability to create easy tunes and explore new musical possibilities. Some of the AI-powered tools that are offering artists and musicians the ability to explore music creation include:

1. Soundraw: Soundraw is a music production tool that creates royalty-free music for creators using AI. It makes it easy to generate soundtracks for various projects, offering a wide range of possibilities for music creation.

2. Dreamtonics Synthesizer V: Dreamtonics Synthesizer V is a tool for creating songs from scratch without any human vocalist. It is great for producers and musicians who want to experiment with new vocals.

3. Aiva: Aiva is a music generator similar to Musenet and Tuney but with different approaches. It offers a novel and completely free method for creating music tracks at the push of a button. The platform uses machine learning to automatically create high-quality music in various styles, including EDM, Hip Hop, Latin, Pop, R&B, and Reggaeton.

4. WavTool: WavTool is a pioneering text-to-music AI tool that offers musicians an innovative approach to music production. Accessible via a web browser, it provides an easy way to generate base melodies, write new songs, and even compose fully AI-generated tracks ready for distribution on platforms like Spotify.

5. Magenta Studio (v1.0): Magenta Studio is a free AI music generator published by Google. It contains a stock of music creativity tools and plugins that are compatible with both MacOS and Windows. Musicians can easily transform a simple melody or riff into a fully composed instrumental piece using Magenta's neural network.

6. Meta's AudioCraft: Meta, the parent company of Facebook, has developed AudioCraft, an AI music tool that offers new possibilities for music creation and sound production.

7. iZotope : iZotope offers AI assistants for music production, providing tools that leverage machine learning to enhance the creative process for musicians and producers.

8. Aiva Technologies: Aiva Technologies is an AI music composition company that provides a platform for creating and customizing original music. Their AI technology allows users to generate unique sound- tracks tailored to their specific needs.

9. Amper Music: Amper Music offers an AI music composition platform that provides tools for creating and customizing original music. Their AI technology allows users to generate unique soundtracks tailored to their specific needs.

These companies and organizations are at the forefront of leveraging AI in music production, sound creation, and music composition, offering new possibilities for artists, musicians, and producers.

Generative AI tools have already begun to revolutionize the way brands create products and interact with customers. By leveraging these tools, creatives and brands can offer personalized and innovative products to their customers, thereby enhancing their creative offerings and providing a unique value proposition. As these tools continue to advance, their role in the creative process will likely become even more pronounced, offering brands and creatives unprecedented opportunities for innovation and artistic exploration.

33 The Future of AI is Hybrid

Hybrid AI refers to systems that combine both artificial intelligence (AI) and human input or decision-making, leveraging the strengths of both to achieve more effective, efficient, or creative outcomes. This approach recognizes that while AI can process and analyze data at incredible speeds and scale, human beings bring nuanced understanding, emotional intelligence, creativity, and ethical judgment that are currently beyond the scope of purely automated systems.

Components of Hybrid AI
1. Artificial Intelligence:

- Machine Learning: AI systems that learn from data and improve over time.
- Natural Language Processing: AI that understands and generates human language.
- Computer Vision: AI that interprets and understands visual information from the world.
- Predictive Analytics: AI that analyzes current and historical data to make predictions.

2. Human Input:

- Decision Making: Humans make final decisions in areas where moral, ethical, or complex subjective judgments are needed.
- Creative Input: Humans provide creative ideas, designs, or insights that AI cannot generate on its own.
- Emotional Intelligence: Human capacity to understand and respond to emotions, a domain where AI is still limited.
- Ethical and Moral Oversight: Ensuring that AI operates within ethical boundaries and societal norms.

Applications of Hybrid AI
1. Healthcare:

AI analyzes medical data and suggests diagnoses or treatments, but doctors make final decisions, considering the patient's overall context, history, and preferences.

2. Business Analytics:

AI processes vast amounts of business data to identify patterns or predict trends, while human analysts use these insights to make strategic decisions.

3. Creative Industries:

In art, music, or literature, AI can generate basic designs or compositions, but human artists infuse these outputs with creative flair and deeper meaning.

4. Customer Service:

AI handles routine inquiries through chatbots, but human agents step in for complex issues requiring empathy and nuanced understanding.

5. Financial Services:

AI assists in analyzing market data and identifying investment opportunities, but financial experts make the final call, considering a wider range of economic factors and client needs.

6. Education:

AI can personalize learning materials based on student performance, but teachers provide guidance, mentorship, and in-depth explanations.

Advantages of Hybrid AI

- Efficiency and Scale: AI handles large-scale data processing and routine tasks, freeing humans for higher-level tasks.
- Accuracy and Reliability: Combines AI's data-processing capabilities with human oversight to reduce errors.
- Creativity and Innovation: Leverages human creativity with AI's ability to generate novel patterns and ideas.
- Ethical Safeguards: Human oversight ensures that AI operates within ethical and legal boundaries.
- Personalization and Contextual Understanding: AI's personalization with human understanding of context and nuance.

Challenges and Considerations

- Integration: Seamlessly integrating AI and human inputs can be technically and organizationally challenging.

- Ethical and Privacy Concerns: Ensuring that AI respects privacy and ethical standards, especially in sensitive fields like healthcare or education.
- Dependence and Skill Loss: Potential for over-reliance on AI, leading to erosion of human skills.
- Bias and Fairness: Addressing biases in AI algorithms and ensuring fairness in decision-making.

In summary, Hybrid AI represents a balanced approach, harnessing the power of AI while retaining the irreplaceable value of human judgment, creativity, and ethical considerations. It's a rapidly evolving field, reflecting an ongoing dialogue between technological capabilities and human needs.

Hybrid AI is particularly important for creatives and can provide them with a significant edge in this evolving era for several key reasons:

Enhanced Creativity and Innovation
1. Complementarity of Skills:

- AI's Strengths: AI excels in analyzing large datasets, identifying patterns, and generating basic creative content (like draft designs, music compositions, etc.) quickly and efficiently.
- Human Creativity: Humans bring unique creative insights, emotional depth, and cultural context that AI lacks. The human touch transforms AI-generated content into nuanced, emotion- ally resonant works.

3. Expanding Creative Horizons:

- AI can suggest novel combinations or ideas that might not occur to a human, pushing creative boundaries and sparking new inspirations.
- Creatives can experiment with AI-generated options, refining and melding these with their vision to create truly innovative art.

Personalization and Customization
1. Tailored Content:
- AI can process user data to create personalized content suggestions, which creatives can then interpret and mold to create deeply resonant and customized artistic outputs.

- This synergy allows for a higher degree of personalization in creative works, from customized storytelling to tailored design products.

Efficiency and Productivity
1. Automating Routine Tasks:
- AI can handle repetitive or time-consuming tasks (like data analysis, basic editing, and pattern generation), freeing creatives to focus on the more nuanced aspects of their work.
- This division of labor increases productivity and allows creatives to undertake more projects or delve deeper into the creative process.

New Opportunities and Business Models
1. Expanding Markets:

- Hybrid AI tools can open up new markets and audiences, as AI-driven analysis can identify untapped niches or emerging trends. Creatives can leverage these insights to create targeted, relevant content.

2. Innovative Business Models:
- AI can enable new forms of artistic expression and interaction, leading to novel business models (e.g., AI-personalized art platforms, AI-driven interactive experiences).
- Creatives can monetize their work in ways that were not possible before, like creating dynamic art pieces that change based on viewer interactions or environmental factors.

Ethical and Responsible Creation
1. Human Oversight:
- In an era increasingly conscious of ethical, cultural, and social implications, human oversight ensures that AI-generated content is responsible and sensitive to these concerns.

- Creatives can guide AI to avoid unintentional biases or inappropriate content, ensuring that the final product aligns with societal values and norms.

Why Creatives Have an Edge
1. Understanding of Human Emotion and Culture:
- Creatives are adept at interpreting human emotions and cultural contexts, which is crucial in tailoring AI outputs to be meaningful and engaging.
- This understanding allows them to modify AI-generated content in ways that resonate on a deeper level with audiences

2. Adaptability and Learning:
- Creatives often excel in learning and adapting to new tools and mediums. The ability to integrate AI into their workflow can set them apart in a technology-driven landscape.
- Their willingness to experiment and learn from AI-generated suggestions or patterns can lead to unique artistic expressions.

3. Ethical and Artistic Judgment:
- Creatives bring a sense of ethics, aesthetics, and artistic judgment to the table, ensuring that the use of AI in creative work is thoughtful, purposeful, and socially conscious.
- They can navigate the complexities of using AI in a way that enhances their work while maintaining artistic integrity and ethical standards.

In conclusion, the era of Hybrid AI presents a landscape rich with opportunities for creatives. By blending their unique human insights with the capabilities of AI, creatives can not only enhance their artistry and efficiency but also pioneer new forms of expression and interaction in the digital age. This synergy of human creativity and AI opens doors to unprecedented possibilities in the creative realm.

34 The Final Stretch - Sustaining Creativity and Success

As creator and educator who has spoken around the world about AI and delivered keynotes at events including Google's Techmakers Event, Dubai's Gitex, and Fast Company's Innovation Summit, I understand the promise and danger presented by rapidly advancing technology. Used wisely, AI can enhance human potential and global prosperity. Used recklessly, it threatens jobs, privacy rights, and more. Charting a wise path forward amidst the unknown requires adaptability, nuanced thinking, and proactive solutions.

My life's work involves equipping the next generation with the mindset and skillset to ride the AI wave rather than be swept away by it. Creative confidence, emotional intelligence, and computational literacy will determine who sinks or swims in the AI- dominated landscape. Beyond job-specific technical skills, young people need assistance developing their distinctly human talents for imagination, strategy, collaboration, communication, and ethical reasoning.

Rather than reactive or alarmist, my vision is grounded in practical optimism. Technological change is inevitable but how we respond lies within our power. AI pioneer Fei-Fei Li of Stanford University wisely states, "I fundamentally believe that if we educate people better, give them better tools for critical thinking, we get a better outcome."

The Role of Education

With a commitment to ongoing training and upskilling, humans maintain the advantage despite AI's superior speed and accuracy at select tasks. We direct the jockey while riding the horse. Education plays a lead role by promoting adaptability, computational literacy, and multidisciplinary critical thinking.

Most importantly, students need early exposure to computer science concepts so they can be informed citizens and innovators. Learning no longer needs to focus on advanced coding skills but rather on a foundational understanding of what AI is and how it works. Analogous to a high school or college biology class, imparting an overview of genetics without requiring students to map DNA.

Interdisciplinary learning will also prove essential. Renowned physicist Stephen Hawking notes, "Everyone can enjoy a life of luxurious leisure if the machine-produced wealth is shared, or most people can end up miserably poor if the machine owners successfully lobby against wealth redistribution. So far, the trend seems to be toward the second option, with technology driving ever-increasing inequality." Here Hawking highlights the importance of exploring AI's ethical implications across disciplines like economics, governance, and moral philosophy rather than pure engineering alone.

Promoting Creativity and Adaptability

Finally, traditional academic subjects must increasingly incorporate creative expression. STEM must make room for arts education. Beyond imparting technical skills, schools exist to nourish young people's humanity. As the Brookings Institution highlights, "The things that make us human – art, music, humor, language, social connections, the search for meaning and purpose, imagination, our ability to do much more than repeat rote tasks – will only become more valuable."

Today's early passion for painting or poetry may manifest later as augmented creativity or design expertise. We rob students of tools for future resilience by narrowly teaching them to standardized tests rather than nurturing their individuality.

Protecting Jobs and Privacy with Wise Governance

Alongside adjusted educational priorities, balanced policy and governance can help smooth the AI transition. Worker protections through retraining programs and basic income schemes recognize those displaced by automation deserve support. Strengthening digital privacy laws helps safeguard human dignity and prevents AI from being weaponized against vulnerable groups.

Rather than a job eliminator, AI may usher in a new craft economy with a premium placed on uniquely human skills like creativity, empathy, and ethics. The World Economic Forum Future of Jobs 2020 report estimates 85 million jobs lost but 97 million jobs gained through 2025 as AI enhances work while allowing redeployment of talent.

A recent McKinsey study suggests AI may not eliminate jobs but rather transform them, with as many as one-third of US workers needing to switch occupations. Through ongoing education and wise policy, we can reduce skills gaps and ease difficult transitions.

The Light Ahead

With proactive preparation, this period of uncertainty can give way to extraordinary possibilities. AI stands to help cure disease, expand access to education, increase productivity, lower costs, and dematerialize work as augmented reality develops. The challenge and opportunity of our time is to guide this technological change toward equitable and sustainable progress.

I often close my keynotes discussing a question posed by young people: "Will everything be okay?" I share this response: "As we stand at the frontier of exponential technological change, nothing is certain except our power to thoughtfully respond. Through compassion, courage, and creativity, we write the next chapter."

There lies my call to action for readers, leaders, and youth. If we face the AI future with adapted skills, ethical responsibility, and creative imagination we may build a world of greater justice, joy, and possibility than previously conceived. The story ahead remains unwritten. Let's take the reins and write something beautiful.

CITATIONS

Part 1 Citations:
[1] https://skimai.com/10-quotes-by-generative-ai-experts/
[2] https://www.supplychaintoday.com/the-best-generative-ai-quotes/
[3] https://www.nisum.com/nisum-knows/top-10-thought-provoking-quotes-from-experts-that-redefine-the-future-of-ai-technology
[4] https://www.forbes.com/sites/bernardmarr/2017/07/25/28-best-quotes-about-artificial-intelligence/
[5] https://bernardmarr.com/28-best-quotes-about-artificial-intelligence/

Part 2 Citations:
[1] https://www.supplychaintoday.com/the-best-generative-ai-quotes/
[2] https://skimai.com/10-quotes-by-generative-ai-experts/
[3] https://www.nisum.com/nisum-knows/top-10-thought-provoking-quotes-from-experts-that-redefine-the-future-of-ai-technology
[4] https://bernardmarr.com/28-best-quotes-about-artificial-intelligence/
[5] https://www.forbes.com/sites/bernardmarr/2017/07/25/28-best-quotes-about-artificial-intelligence/

Part 3 Citations:
[1] https://www.elegantthemes.com/blog/marketing/best-ai-story-generators
[2] https://juliety.com/ai-book-writing-software
[3] https://selfpublishing.com/ai-editor/
[4] https://deepgram.com/ai-apps/novelflow
[5] https://www.canva.com/magic-write/

Part 4 Citations:
[1] https://selfpublishing.com/ai-editor/
[2] https://juliety.com/ai-book-writing-software

[3] https://en.wikipedia.org/wiki/Readability
[4] https://hackmd.io/@aesthetic-programming/Notes

Part 5 Citations:
[1] https://www.youtube.com/watch?v=KqTnmNjkaec
[2] https://nerdynovelist.com/24-chapter-novel-outline/
[3] https://louisadeasey.com/how-to-write-chapter-outlines/
[4] https://self-publishingschool.com/parts-of-a-book/
[5] https://hackmd.io/@aesthetic-programming/Notes

[1] https://www.youtube.com/watch?v=KqTnmNjkaec
[2] https://nerdynovelist.com/24-chapter-novel-outline/
[3] https://www.dabblewriter.com/articles/chatgpt-for-fiction
[4] https://louisadeasey.com/how-to-write-chapter-outlines/
[5] https://hackmd.io/@aesthetic-programming/Notes
[6] https://www.goldcast.io/blog-post/ai-tools-to-boost-creativity
[7] https://slashdot.org/software/p/Sudowrite/alternatives
[8] https://www.canva.com/magic-write/

About The Author

Named one of the Most Inspirational Women of Web3 and AI, Nova Lorraine is an acclaimed Fashion Designer and Futurist. Renowned for her design prowess, she's been featured in Forbes, Inc., Italian Vogue, TV shows like "The View", and fashion designs gracing the stage of "Oprah". Nova recently celebrated being the first Jamaican fashion designer to have her art land on the moon. She also was recently selected as a Top Voice in AI by LinkedIn. Nova enjoys using fashion, art, and storytelling to inspire and educate.

With 15+ years in fashion and media, Nova's accolades extend to international speaking engagements and published authorship. She has received noteworthy awards such as the Web3 Creator Future Award, the Metaverse Champion Award, and the esteemed LAMINA1 NFT Artist Award, cementing her as a trailblazer in both artistic and digital domains. Named a Top 100 Women of the Future, Nova's impact in the Metaverse was also acknowledged by BEYA, and she also serves as a Hult Prize Judge.

In her free time, Nova enjoys running, reading, and traveling with her family.

Made in the USA
Middletown, DE
20 October 2024